Werner Burkhardt

First Steps in
Maple

Springer-Verlag
London Berlin Heidelberg New York
Paris Tokyo Hong Kong
Barcelona Budapest

Werner Burkhardt
Talstrasse 42
68259 Mannheim
Germany

ISBN 3–540–19874–1 Springer-Verlag Berlin Heidelberg New York
ISBN 0–387–19874–1 Springer-Verlag New York Berlin Heidelberg

Originally published in German under the title: Erste Schritte mit Maple
Copyright © Springer-Verlag Berlin Heidelberg 1994.
All Rights Reserved.

Translation by Malcolm Stewart

British Library Cataloguing in Publication Data
A catalogue record for this book is available from the British Library

Library of Congress Cataloging-in-Publication Data
A catalog record for this book is available from the Library of Congress

© Springer-Verlag London Limited 1994

Typeset by Richard Powell Editorial and Production Services,
Basingstoke RG22 4TX
Printed by Athenæum Press Ltd, Gateshead, England
34/3830–543210 (printed on acid-free paper)

First Steps in Maple

Contents

Preface

Before the use of computers, that is, before 1950, a mathematical calculation was a mixture of numerical and analytical manipulations. The example of the moonbeam calculations made by Delaunay in the last century shows clearly that this procedure could be very time-consuming: he took 10 years to produce his calculations, and a further 10 years to check them!

We can neither contemplate nor provide such long-winded dedication to a problem in our computer-filled world. Through the introduction of electronic computer systems many problems can be prepared numerically and then worked out, with the results being obtained much more quickly by these new methods than by the older methods. As a result of the success of such methods many scientists today regard the concepts of numerical calculation and scientific calculation as synonymous. Unfortunately, though, numerical calculation has some disadvantages:

- Rounding errors affect the results.
- Problems that are analytically exactly solvable are only solved approximately by numerical methods. Thus the structure of the numerical solution is often not clearly recognisable.

Because of these disadvantages, attempts were made to reconstruct on computers the pencil and paper methods used by everyone before the introduction of computers. The first attempts are to be found in the work of Kahrimanian and Nolen, who in 1953 published an article on symbolic differentiation in computer systems. In the 1960s some computer algebra systems, such as Reduce, MACSYMA, SCRATCHPAD (now Axiom), etc., were developed for main-frames. At the end of the 1970s the first computer algebra systems for PCs appeared; these were criticised by some for requiring as much time as paper calculations, even though they lightened the burden of calculation, largely because of the need to learn the programming language and interpret the results. With the increasing power and productivity of PCs it nevertheless also became possible to implement more user-friendly computer algebra systems on PCs. *Maple* is one of these systems, and its development goes back to around 1980.

At this time it was becoming increasingly clear how important computer algebra systems were in science, technology and mathematics, for the solution of large systems of differential equations, the investigation of problems in fluid mechanics, the investigation of highly symmetrical groups, and so on. This prompted an examination at Waterloo University, Canada, of what was available on the market by way of computer algebra systems to meet the requirements of the University. The survey revealed that none of the available systems met their requirements. One reason for the rejection was the software technology used to produce those packages available at that time. The University of Waterloo therefore set up its own group that would use the technology of the 1980s instead of that of the 1960s to create a new computer algebra system. This was the start of the specification and implementation of a new mathematical programming language, called *Maple* after the Canadian national emblem. The success of this group may now be appreciated. The main program is very compact (about 20 000 lines of C code), which means that it can be compiled on almost all computer platforms. It contains the standard input and output structures, number arithmetic and algorithms for the simplification of terms. Everything else is written in the integrated *Maple* language and is loaded when required. Thus *Maple* places lower demands on working storage than other computer algebra systems.

The development and maintenance of the program was carried out under the UNIX operating system, so that it can be used on all computers that have UNIX installed. In addition, the following operating systems are supported: 386 DOS/Windows, Macintosh Finder, DEC VMS, IBM VM/CMS and Amiga DOS. As the number of available operating systems continues to grow, it can be assumed that *Maple* is available for most computers. The current version is *Maple* V Release 2, with further updates in preparation.

The present book contains an introduction to *Maple* that provides the basic knowledge required to use the package. This knowledge is conveyed by means of examples based on numerous questions from school and college mathematics; at the end of each chapter problems are included to test the reader's knowledge (solutions are given at the end of the book). In selecting the examples, emphasis was placed on the following points:

- Relevance to applications
- Illustrative of the capabilities (and limitations) of *Maple*

Because of this choice of examples the book is especially suitable for the following:

- Self-study users of computer algebra systems
- Courses in *Maple* in schools and colleges
- Scientific mathematical instruction at university level

In conclusion I should like to thank Mr J. Lammarsch for his stimulation and encouragement to write this book. My thanks too to Mrs Luzia Dietsche of DANTE e.V., to whom I frequently took my questions about LATEX, and who always helped me on my way. My appreciation too goes to Springer-Verlag, in particular to Dr Barabas and Dr Rossbach. Finally, I should like to thank my family, who showed such understanding during the time that I was preoccupied with this book.

Werner Burkhardt

1 Introduction

Like many other computer-based algebra systems, *Maple* can also function as an input–output system; that is, it receives a task as input and provides the solution as output. To allow *Maple* to be used on several computers, it was programmed in three parts:

1. The kernel, which is the same on all computers.
2. The front end, which is machine dependent.
3. The library, which in *Maple* contains written commands and programs. This is identical on all machines.

This division into three parts is first of all efficient for the implementation and programming of *Maple*, since only the user interface needs to be specifically programmed. The kernel is written in a macro language (called Margay) from the source text of which input text for the C programming language can be produced.

User interfaces may broadly be categorised as text-oriented or graphics-oriented (notebooks). As it would exceed the limits of this book to describe in detail all user levels/interfaces, we shall restrict ourselves to the input techniques that are possible on all machines. The inputs are shown in Courier typewriter face, while the outputs appear in mathematical notation. This description is the same as the display on almost all computers, especially those with graphics interfaces. In text-based interfaces *Maple* attempts to reproduce this form of display as far as possible. Later parts of this book consist of input and output dialogues, in which only the parts after the 'greater than' symbol are to be taken as the input data. The following section gives some examples.

1.1 Starting *Maple*

The following description assumes that a complete *Maple* system is installed. Appendix 1 describes the installation of *Maple* on PCs. As *Maple* is available for a great many computers and operating systems with the most disparate interfaces, the following table shows the start commands for the most common computers and operating systems.

1

Computer/Operating system	How to start *Maple*
Macintosh, NeXT, MS Windows	Select and click the *Maple* symbol.
MS-DOS, Unix	Input the `maple` command. The command must be confirmed by striking the `Return` key.
X Window systems and DEC Windows	Input the `xmaple` command. The command must be confirmed by striking the `Return` key.
SunView	Input the `svmaple` command. The command must be confirmed by striking the `Return` key.

If *Maple* cannot be started with one of these commands, the correct command will need to be found from the accompanying manuals.

Once *Maple* has successfully started, a message appears, depending on the system and version number, terminating with the input prompt > or •. In the following text the input prompt is shown by the 'greater than' symbol (>). At this prompt the user can make the desired input to which *Maple* will respond. This input must be confirmed by striking the RETURN key (with Macintosh and NeXT systems the Enter key on the numeric pad must be used). For example:

Screen display:

>

Inputting 8+17 produces on the next line of the screen:

> 8+17

On striking the RETURN key the screen shows:

>

This output indicates that the command for *Maple* is not yet terminated and it is waiting for further input. In *Maple* the end of a command is indicated by a semicolon. After inputting a semicolon and striking the RETURN key the complete screen display appears as follows:

> 8+17
> ;
                    25
>

As can be seen, the output is indented and is followed by the prompt (>) for the next input on the line below.

In the examples from now on the semicolon at the end of the input should not be forgotten. The correct input for the previous example is therefore 8+17;.

When we wish to work with *Maple*, we need commands that may be found in the manuals that are supplied with the package. However, since it is very tedious and time-consuming to look up commands in manuals, a friendly help system has been developed for each version of the package for use with all operating systems and computers. It takes the form described below.

To obtain help, the user keys a single question mark at the prompt. On striking RETURN the following summary is displayed through which one can browse:

```
FUNCTION: help — descriptions of systems, datatypes,
and functions

CALLING SEQUENCE:
    ?topic  or  ?topic,subtopic  or  ?topic[subtopic]  or
    help(topic)      or      help(topic,subtopic)      or
    help(topic[subtopic])

SYNOPSIS:
    ?intro                    introduction to Maple
    ?library                  Maple library functions
                                and procedures
    ?index                    list of all help
                                categories
    ?index,<category>         list of help files on
                                specific topics
    ?<topic>                  explanation of a specific
                                topic
    ?<topic>,<subtopic>       explanation of a subtopic
                                under a topic
    ?distribution             for information on how to
                                obtain Maple
    ?copyright                for information about
                                copyrights
    ...

SEE ALSO:   keywords, quotes, colons, quit, example,
scg, distribution, TEXT
```

The following input will provide an overview of the help obtainable from `Maple`:

```
< ?index

HELP FOR: Index of help descriptions

CALLING SEQUENCE:
    ?index[<category>]    or    help(index, <category>);

SYNOPSIS:
- The following categories of topics are available in
the help subsystem.
```

library	Index of descriptions for standard library functions
packages	Index of descriptions for library packages of functions
libmisc	Index of descriptions for miscellaneous lib functions
statements	Index of descriptions for Maple statements
expressions	Index of descriptions for Maple expressions
datatypes	Index of descriptions for Maple datatypes
tables	Index of descriptions for tables and arrays in Maple
procedures	Index of descriptions for Maple procedures
misc	Index of descriptions for miscellaneous facilities

Information about the individual subheadings can be obtained here by inputting the question mark, followed by the subhead item. For example, the following input will provide information about allowable assignments:

```
> ?statements
```

HELP FOR: Index of descriptions for Maple statements

SYNOPSIS:
- There are eight types of statements in Maple. See ?topic for any of the following topics:

assignment do empty expression if quit
read save

- In an interactive Maple session, each statement must be terminated with a semicolon (;) or a colon (:) before the statement will be executed. The only exception is the quit statement, which does not require a punctuation mark.

SEE ALSO: keywords, colonc, break, next, return, error

The input ?quit provides a description of the quit command. The display in the help windows that appear on the monitor is similar to that found in the manuals. Generally, the information on the screen is more up to date than that found in the manuals. Now the input:

```
> ?quit
```

HELP FOR: The quit statement

SYNOPSIS:
- Any one of: quit, done, stop

- The quit statement terminates the Maple session and returns the user to the system level from which Maple was entered.

- In many implementations of Maple, hitting the break/interrupt key twice in rapid succession, or some similar system-specific sequence, will also terminate a Maple session.

Even when errors occur, caused by the incorrect use of a command or similar, *Maple* offers help. Examples in the following sections will illustrate how this is done.

From the last display output the reader will see that the `quit` command is used to end a *Maple* session.

To start *Maple*	`maple` (or similar)
To end a command	`;`(semicolon)
To confirm input	`RETURN`
To request help	`?concept`
To quit *Maple*	`quit`

Starting and ending Maple

1.2 Calculating with numbers

As the previous section showed, *Maple* can be used as a pocket calculator. But of course much larger numbers can be manipulated:

```
> 987543321234567890*12341234567987654-987678965432345;
```

$$121875037734053854697791 80579397715$$

Most pocket calculators would not be able to provide all the digits of this solution.

Normally in mathematics it is customary to insert a space instead of the multiplication sign. However, *Maple* will not accept input of this kind. The multiplication sign * must be written.

Of course, *Maple* also handles division:

```
> 5/17;
```

$$5/17$$

This output is unusual, as here one would have expected to see a decimal number, as on a pocket calculator. (Note that in this book a decimal number is understood to be a number that can be represented with the digits 0 to 9 and the decimal point.) Because *Maple* is a computer algebraic system that calculates everything exactly, the same display is used for all numbers, that is, there is no decimal approximation, unless this is specifically requested.

There is the possibility of producing a decimal number from the numerator and denominator of the above fraction. This method of course also works if both are input as decimal numbers:

```
> 5./17;
```

$$.2941176471$$

Here *Maple* assumes that a number is input as a decimal and therefore outputs the result as a decimal number.

The other possibility is to use the *Maple* evalf command. This command calculates a decimal approximation for the argument:

```
> evalf(5/17);
```

$$.2941176471$$

The number of decimal places normally provided as output depends on the computer and the basic precision stipulated. If more places are required (say 50), this can be specified with the Digits command:

```
> Digits:=50;
```

$$Digits := 50$$

Recalculating 5/17 with evalf produces the required number of decimal places:

```
> evalf(5/17);
```

$$.29411764705882352941176470588235294117647058823529$$

For the following calculations the number of decimal places is once again reduced:

```
> Digits:=10:
```

Here the input is terminated with a colon instead of a semicolon. Thus the output of Digits :=10 is underlined. If only one calculation with a larger number of decimal places is to be carried out, this input may be passed as second argument to the evalf command. Thus we have for the last calculation:

```
> evalf(5/17,50);
```

$$.29411764705882352941176470588235294117647058823529$$

Now follows an example of calculating with brackets/parentheses:

```
> (8+12)/7;
```

Again, a decimal approximation can be obtained with the `evalf` command.

Now, an example of raising to a power. The inventor of chess requested as payment from his king $2^{64} - 1$ grains of corn. This number can be calculated exactly with *Maple*:

```
> 2^64-1;
```

$$18446744073709551615$$

Many pocket calculators allow factorials to be calculated; unfortunately, most calculators cannot cope with a number greater than 69!. Here is an example of a rather large number:

```
> 101!;
```

94259477598383594208516231244829367495623127947025437683278\
89353416977599316221476503087861591808346911623490003549599\
58336970630260326400000000000000000000000000000\

The backslash (\) in this output is used as a separator, to indicate that the output continues on the next line.

The number 101! is very easy to factorise. For this the *Maple* `factor` command is used.

Here is an example:

```
> factor(");
```

94259477598383594208516231244829367495623127947025437683278\
93534169775993162214765030878615918083469116234900035495995\
33697063026032640000000000000000000000000000\

In the input the previous result was retrieved with the double quote symbol, in order to save labour and calculating time. It is possible to retrieve even earlier results by inputting multiple double quotes (double, triple, etc.).

From the output we can see that *Maple* recognises the `factor` command — it would otherwise appear again in the output — but the required transformation is not carried out. To obtain more information the help function (`?factor`) is invoked. Here is an extract:

```
SYNOPSIS:
-  The  function  factor  computes  the  factorization  of  a
multivariate polynomial with integer, rational, or algebraic
number coefficients.

SEE  ALSO:     ifactor,  Factor,  AFactor,  factors,  sqrfree,
collect, galois, irreduc, roots
```

This means that the `factor` command is only used on polynomials and further information can be found under other keywords. `ifactor` is one of these. The following are some actual extracts from the associated help text:

```
FUNCTION: ifactor — integer factorization

CALLING SEQUENCE:
    ifactor(n)
    ifactor(n, method)

PARAMETERS:
    n       — integer or a rational
    method  — (optional) name of base method for factoring

SYNOPSIS:
- ifactor returns the complete integer factorization of n.

EXAMPLES:
> ifactor( 60 );
```

$$2$$
$$(2)\ (3)\ (5)$$

The example shows the call command for factorising a number:

```
> ifactor(101!);
```

$$(2)^{97}\ (3)^{48}\ (5)^{24}\ (7)^{16}\ (11)^{9}\ (13)^{7}\ (17)^{5}\ (19)^{5}\ (23)^{4}$$
$$(29)^{3}\ (31)^{3}\ (37)^{2}\ (41)^{2}\ (43)^{2}\ (47)^{2}\ (53)\ (59)\ (61)$$
$$(67)\ (71)\ (73)\ (79)\ (83)\ (89)\ (97)\ (101)$$

This output illustrates the structure of *Maple* commands.

- Almost all *Maple* commands start with a lower case letter.
- If a command consists of several words or abbreviations, these are joined together with no intervening space; new words start with a lower case letter.
- The arguments of a command are enclosed within parentheses.
- Every command must terminate with a semicolon (;) or a colon (:).

Structure of Maple commands

- Addition, subtraction, multiplication and division are input to the computer using the usual symbols (+ − * /).
- For exponentiation/raising to powers the ^ symbol is used.
- For factorials the ! symbol is used.
- To obtain decimal approximations for a value the `evalf` command is invoked.
- The number of required decimal places is permanently altered by the `Digits` command. (Thus, inputting `Digits:=100;` will cause subsequent decimal numbers to be shown to 100 places.)
- The double quote (") retrieves the last result or references it.
- The paired double quote ("") retrieves the penultimate result, and so on. On most systems it is possible to go up to three quotes.
- Appending a colon to an input line causes the output to be underlined.

Summary of calculation rules

1.3 Calculating with real numbers and functions

As already mentioned, *Maple* attempts to calculate exactly. This means that fractions are only reduced; they are not transformed into decimal numbers. This section will describe the effect that this has on calculating with roots, logarithms and functions.

First, a few examples of calculating with roots. The *Maple* command for the square root is sqrt.

Exact calculation of $\sqrt{3}\sqrt{7}$:

```
> sqrt(3)*sqrt(7);
```

$$\sqrt{3}\sqrt{7}$$

Here the output appears in factorised form. From the point of view of the authors of *Maple* this is the simplest representation. Both roots can be merged with the combine command:

```
> combine(");
```

$$\sqrt{21}$$

Because $\sqrt{21}$ can neither be represented as a whole number, nor as a fraction with a whole number numerator and denominator, the result remains as shown.

The next two examples show how *Maple* calculates roots from sums. First,
```
> sqrt(576+49);
```

$$\sqrt{576+49}$$

$$25$$

First, the argument of the root function is calculated. Because it is a square, the root is also determined. The same explanation goes for

$$\sqrt{\frac{81}{16} - 2}:$$

```
> sqrt(81/16-2);
```

$$7/4$$

From these examples we can see that *Maple* attempts to determine the result according to the normal rules for the calculation of roots. For this reason the first example yields the result $\sqrt{21}$. A decimal approximation may be obtained by inserting the decimal point after the corresponding number:

```
> sqrt(3.)*sqrt(7);
```

$$1.732050808\sqrt{7}$$

Because only the argument of the first root is designated as a decimal number, only this is transformed into a decimal. The second root remains as an exact number. The following example shows a way of obtaining a decimal approximation of the result. Instead, the evalf command can also be used. (Both methods give the same result to the same number of decimal places.)

```
> sqrt(3.)*sqrt(7.);
```

$$4.582575696$$

```
> evalf(sqrt(3)*sqrt(7));
```

$$4.582575696$$

To calculate higher roots ($\sqrt[3]{x}$...) fractional exponents must be used ($\sqrt[n]{x} = x^{1/n}$).

For logarithms there are the log and ln commands for natural logarithms (with the Euler number e as base) and log[Basis] for logarithms to a required base. When inputting the log[Basis](x) command the word Basis must first be replaced by a number and x by a variable or a number. The following examples illustrate the use of these commands:

```
> ln(E^5);
```

As can be seen, E is the *Maple* representation of the Euler number *e*.

```
> ln(200);
```

$$\ln(200)$$

Because 200 is not a rational power of *e*, the exact solution remains as ln200. The simplify command allows the result to be simplified with the aid of the rules of logarithms:

```
> simplify(");
```

$$3\ln(2) + 2\ln(5)$$

A decimal approximation:

```
> ln(200.);
```

$$5.298317367$$

The same pattern of rules applies here as with roots for the representation of expressions in *Maple*.

Many users, chemists, for example, prefer logarithms to the base 10. Here the log[Basis] command can be used. The following is an example of the calculation of the logarithm of 10 000 to the base 10:

```
> log[10](10000);
```

$$\frac{\ln(10000)}{\ln(10)}$$

From the appearance of the output we can see that *Maple* works internally with natural logarithms, since the output is displayed as natural logarithms. To calculate the result, the simplify command must be used:

```
> simplify(");
```

$$4$$

For logarithms to the base 10 *Maple* offers the log10 command. This command is found in that part of the *Maple* command library which is not automatically loaded. It therefore needs to be read in by the readlib command:

```
> readlib(log10):
> log10(10000);
```

$$\frac{\ln(10000)}{\ln(10)}$$

```
> simplify(");
```

4

This makes it clear that the commands `log10` and `log(10)` behave in the same way. For logarithms to other bases the `log[Basis]` command is used. Here is an example to base 2:

```
> log[2](8);
```

$$\frac{\ln(8)}{\ln(2)}$$

```
>simplify(");
```

3

For the exponential function to base *e Maple* recognises `E^x` and `exp(x)`. Either can be used.

Root function($\sqrt{x}$)	`sqrt(x)`
Exponential function (e^x)	`exp(x)` or `E^x`
Natural logarithmic function (ln x)	`ln(x)`
Logarithmic function to base b ($\log_b x$)	`log[Basis](x)`

Functions in Maple

The following commands are available for solving trigonometric functions:

Sine function (sin x)	`sin(x)`
Cosine function (cos x)	`cos(x)`
Tangent function (tan x)	`tan(x)`
Cotangent function (cot x)	`cot(x)`
Secant function (sec x)	`sec(x)`
Cosecant function (csc x)	`csc(x)`

Trigonometric functions in Maple

When one of these functions is called, *Maple* expects the argument to be input within parentheses. Of course, all trigonometric functions are available as inverse functions. The names of the inverse functions are formed by prefixing the function name with the `arc` syllable. Thus, `arccot` is the inverse function of the cotangent function.

The number π is obtained by inputting `Pi`. In the following examples the display rules described above apply. *Maple* calculates precisely the trigonometric functions for special values such as $\pi/6$, $\pi/4$, $\pi/3$, etc., that is, in the form of roots and fractions. If this is not possible, *Maple* does not alter the input and, if necessary, continues to calculate further with this precise result. If a decimal approximation for the value of the trigonometric function is required, this must be indicated by appending the decimal point or by using the `evalf` function:

```
> sin(Pi/4);
```

$$\frac{1}{2}\sqrt{2}$$

```
> tan(3*Pi/4);
```

$$-1$$

```
> cos(4);
```

$$\cos(4)$$

```
> cos(4.);
```

$$-.6536436209$$

```
> arctan(1);
```

$$\frac{1}{4}\pi$$

```
> arcsin(1/2);
```

$$\frac{1}{6}\pi$$

Consider in these examples how the output is achieved. Because trigonometric functions are often required for angles in the measurement of gradients, the angle input must be converted from `degrees` into `radians`. For this the `convert` command is used. Thus, cos 150° is calculated by:

```
> cos(convert(150*degrees,radians));
```

$$-\frac{1}{2}\sqrt{3}$$

1.4   Calculating with complex numbers and functions

To represent complex numbers, the imaginary unit i is used, with $i^2 = -1$. In *Maple* this is represented by I. Complex numbers are input in the form a+ I*b or a+ b*I. Now, an example of the basic rules:

```
> (3+5*I)*(7+6*I);
```

$$(3 + 5I)(7 + 6I)$$

It can be seen that the input is neither simplified nor evaluated. The evalc command is needed for this. The next examples illustrate its syntax and use:

```
> evalc((3+5*I)*(7+6*I));
```

$$-9 + 53I$$

```
> evalc(12/(3+5*I));
```

$$\frac{18}{17} - \frac{30I}{17}$$

```
> evalc((sqrt(2)+sqrt(3)*I)/(sqrt(2)-sqrt(3)*I));
```

$$-\frac{1}{5} + \frac{2\sqrt{2}\sqrt{3}\,I}{5}$$

To manipulate complex numbers there are several commands available: Re, Im, conjugate, abs, polar. Examples of these follow.

To calculate the real part:

```
> Re(E+17*I);
```

$$E$$

To calculate the imaginary part:

```
> Im(E+17*I);
```

17

To calculate the complex conjugate:

```
> conjugate(E+17*I);
```

$$E - 17I$$

To calculate the modulus:

```
> abs(E+17*I);
```

$$\sqrt{E^2 + 289}$$

To calculate arguments with the Euler representation $e^{i\phi}$ of a complex number, the `arctan` command with two arguments — the real and the imaginary parts of the complex number — is invoked:

```
> arctan(17,E);
```

$$\arctan(17/E)$$

To obtain a decimal approximation:

```
> evalf(");
```

$$.1585567145$$

It is often necessary to convert complex numbers from cartesian to polar coordinate representation, and vice versa. This can be done with the `convert` command. To convert a complex number into polar coordinates:

```
> convert(2+2*I,polar);
```

$$polar(2\sqrt{2}, \frac{\pi}{4})$$

Here we can see that the `polar` command outputs the modulus as first argument and as second the argument of the complex number. Invoking the `evalc` command on `polar` produces the cartesian representation:

```
> evalc(polar(3,3*Pi/4));
```

$$-\frac{3}{2}\sqrt{2} + \frac{3}{2}I\sqrt{2}$$

Simplification of the examples to `Re`, `Im` ... is not directly carried by all versions of *Maple*. If it is not, the result must be simplified with the evalc command.

The following commands are available for the manipulation of complex numbers:

Representation	x + I*y or x + y*I
Simplification	evalc
Real part	Re(z)
Imaginary part	Im(z)
Modulus	abs(z)
Argument	arctan(Re(z),Im(z))
Complex conjugate	conjugate(z)
Representation in polar coordinates	convert(z,polar) or polar(z)
Conversion into cartesian coordinates	evalc(polar(*total, argument*))
z : complex number	

The functions that were examined in the previous section can also be applied to complex arguments.

Complex functions

1.5   Problems

1. Find the prime factors of 2^{45} − 1.
2. Calculate $\sqrt{17}\sqrt{68}$.
3. Calculate ln335 as well as a decimal approximation for the value.
4. Calculate $\log_4 2048$.
5. Calculate sin 135° as well as a decimal approximation for the value.
6. Calculate the real part of the complex number $5 - 5i$.
7. Calculate the imaginary part of $5 - 5i$.
8. Calculate the modulus of $5 - 5i$.
9. Calculate the argument of $5 - 5i$.

2 Term transformations

2.1 Calculating with symbols

The facilities of *Maple* outlined in the previous chapter are those of a very useful pocket calculator. The additional feature that distinguishes computer algebra systems such as *Maple* is that they can calculate with symbols (variables, letters, etc.). Some indication of what calculating with symbols means was given in the previous chapter in the handling of function values. *Maple* calculated $\sqrt{3}\sqrt{7}$ as $\sqrt{21}$, and not 4.582575695, as would be the case with a pocket calculator. Here is an example with symbols:

```
> 4*x+17*b-33*x+14*b+51*x;
```

$$22x + 31b$$

These examples show that *Maple* can operate with symbols as well as numbers. We shall see whether it also copes with the basic calculus for symbols:

```
> (3*x+7)*(5*x+a);
```

$$(3x + 7)(5x + a)$$

This example shows that *Maple* returns the input in unaltered form, but does not carry out the desired calculation. To achieve this, as with complex terms, further commands are required; these will be discussed in the following sections.

In addition, we can see from this example that *Maple* distinguishes precisely between the data types for symbols and numbers. In *Maple* symbols are a sequence of letters, digits and underlines (_) up to a length of 499 characters, where the first character must be a letter. These are handled as independent objects whose values can be assigned. Value assignment in *Maple* is carried out by a colon followed by an 'equals' sign (:=). (In *Maple* the simple 'equals' sign is used for comparisons.)

```
> x:=17;
```

$$x := 17$$

This assigns the value 17 to the variable x. The next example shows the calculation of the term $x - 15$:

```
> x-15;
```

2

The output shows that the variable x is replaced by the value 17. Another example:

```
> x^2-33*x+4;
```

$$-268$$

Since this last term will be considered further, it will be assigned to a variable called TERM. This word is written in upper case, to avoid confusion with *Maple* descriptors, since these generally begin with a lower case letter. This convention will be adopted throughout the remainder of this book for user-defined descriptors:

```
> TERM:=x^2-33*x+4;
```

$$TERM := -268$$

The term was correctly evaluated with the value of 17 for the variable x. Now, an example with another x value. First, x is assigned the value 5 and the term is evaluated:

```
> x:=5;
```

$$x := 5$$

```
> TERM;
```

$$-268$$

From the result we can see that on the assignment of the variable TERM it was not the term $x^2 - 33 * x + 4$; that was evaluated, but the value of this term for $x = 17$ was output. This shows the next direct evaluation for $x = 5$:

```
> 5^2-33*5+4;
```

$$-136$$

In order to re-establish clear output conditions, all definitions are cancelled. To this end every variable has its symbol assigned to it, which is enclosed within simple single quotes. To clear the assignment for x:

```
> x:='x';
```

$$x := x$$

To clear the assignment for the variable TERM:

```
> TERM:='TERM';
```

TERM := TERM

The command `assigned` allows it to be tested whether a value has been assigned to a variable. The response is obtained through input of the variable:

```
> assigned(x);
```

false

```
> x;
```

x

The outputs show that the variables have no assigned value. Now, a further attempt to evaluate a term with different values for the variables. Because in the previous example first *x* and then TERM were assigned, we now take the opposite approach:

```
> TERM:=x^2-33*x+4;
```

$$TERM := x^2 - 33x + 4$$

```
> x:=17;
```

$$x := 17$$

```
> TERM;
```

$$-268$$

```
> x:=5;
```

$$x := 5$$

```
> TERM;
```

$$-136$$

By this means the evaluation of the term for different values of *x* could be obtained. In the first procedure we speak of an early binding of the variable (before the assignment of the term); in the second, there is late binding of the variable (after assignment of the term). For this reason, it is important before evaluating terms to ascertain whether the variables that are contained in the term already have an assigned value.

Assignment of a value to a variable $x := value$
Clearing of assignments $x =' x '$
Interrogation of assignments x
Test whether variable assigned   assigned(x)

- Check thoroughly the values of variables contained in a term before evaluating it.
- Consider carefully which term to assign first and which term to assign later, especially when one depends on the other.

Assignment of variables

2.2 Calculating with rational integral terms

As mentioned in the previous section, *Maple* commands are used to multiply out an expression within parentheses. One of these commands is expand( ). Here is a first example:

```
> expand((41*x+37)*(14*x-43*a));
```

$$574x^2 - 1763xa + 518x - 1591a$$

Now, two more extensive examples:

```
> expand((x+E)^9);
```

$$x^9 + 9x^8e + 36x^7e^2 + 84x^6e^3 + 126x^5e^4 +$$
$$126x^4e^5 + 84x^3e^6 + 36x^2e^7 + 9xe^8 + e^9$$

```
> expand((x+41*a-37)^6;
```

$$28112415x^2 + 2305218030xa - 416063742x - 17058613422a +$$
$$x^6 - 222x^5 + 20535x^4 - 1013060x^3 + 4750104241a^6 +$$
$$2565726409 + 47256969615a^2 - 124606380x^2a - 5108861580xa^2 +$$
$$3367740x^3a + 207116010x^2a^2 + 5661170940xa^3 - 45510x^{4a} -$$
$$3731820x^3a^2 - 153004620x^2a^3 - 3136594710xa^4 + 246x^5a +$$
$$25215x^4a^2 + 1378420x^3a^3 + 42386415x^2a^4 + 695137206xa^5 -$$
$$69821108260a^3 + 58027002135a^4 - 25720076622a^5$$

The calculations for these examples are carried out very quickly; however, because of its length, the output is somewhat obscure. For many calculations often only the first and/or last terms (operands) are needed. In such cases the command op can be used. To illustrate this command we shall define a polynomial. To ensure that the single terms are sorted alphabetically and not according to the location in memory, the sort command is appended to the result:

```
> POLYNOMIAL:=sort(expand((x+1)^105)):
```

The colon at the end of the input suppresses output of the result. Next the first and then the first three terms are determined:

```
> op(1,POLYNOMIAL);
```

$$x^{105}$$

```
> op(1..3,POLYNOMIAL);
```

$$x^{105}, 105x^{104}, 5460x^{103}$$

We can just as easily obtain, for example, the 100th term or all terms between the 45th and the 73rd. To establish how many terms an expression contains, the nops command is used:

```
> nops(POLYNOMIAL);
```

$$106$$

The degree command calculates the degree of a polynomial:

```
> degree(POLYNOMIAL);
```

$$105$$

To determine the coefficient of the leading or lowest power of a variable the commands lcoeff and tcoeff are available. The coeff command yields the coefficient of a given power. As these commands may also be used on polynomials with several variables — called multivariate polynomials — a polynomial (POLYNOMIAL1) with two variables is defined:

```
> POLYNOMIAL1:=sort(expand((2*x-y+3)^4*(x-3*y+5)^3)):
> lcoeff(POLYNOMIAL1);
```

$$16$$

```
> lcoeff(POLYNOMIAL1,X);
```

$$16$$

```
> lcoeff(POLYNOMIAL1),y):
```

$$-27$$

```
> tcoeff(POLYNOMIAL1);
```

$$10125$$

```
> tcoeff(POYNOMIAL1,x);
```

$$-27y^7 +459y^6 -3303y^5 +13031y^4 -30417y^3 +41985y^2 -31725y +10125$$

```
> tcoeff(POLYNOMIAL1,y);
```

$$16x^7 +336x^6 +2856x^5 +12656x^4 +31521x^3 +44415x^2 +33075x +10125$$

```
> coeff(POLYNOMIAL1,x^3);
```

$$1585y^4 - 13740y^3 + 43830y^2 - 61132y + 31521$$

From these examples we can see that the commands lcoeff and tcoeff can be called with or without variables. When called without variables, the variable coefficients are always input; these appear first in the given order, usually alphabetical.

Hitherto the multiplying out and summarising of rational integral terms has been shown in full. However, we often also need the problem to be solved from the point of view of obtaining the factors of a term. Here the factor command is used. The factors of the term $x^3 - 7x^2 + 7x + 15$ are obtained by:

```
> factor(X^3-7*x^2+7*x+14);
```

$$(x + 1)(x - 3)(x - 5)$$

```
> factor(41*x^3+43*x^2+82*x+86);
```

$$(x^2 + 2)(41x + 43)$$

This display contains only factors with real coefficients. To obtain all (including complex) factors, we must provide more data for the factor command. In this case, we need to provide the solutions of the equation $x^2 + 2 = 0$, that is, $\pm I$ $\sqrt{(2)}$. (For difficult terms, chapter 4 shows how *Maple* can help to obtain the solutions.) This method seems complicated; but its true advantage is shown when factorising any algebraic expressions. (This material is usually covered in the first high school semester.)

```
> factor(41*x^3+43*x^2+82*x+86,I*sqrt(2));
```

$$(x - I \sqrt{2})(x + I \sqrt{2})(41x + 43)$$

Expand (multiply out, summarise) a term	`expand( `*expr*` )`
Factorise a term with real factors	`factor( `*expr, options*` )`
Factorise a term for a given expression	`Factor( `*expr, K*` )`
Coefficients of a variable	`coeff( `*expr, var*` )`
Largest coefficient of a variable	`lcoeff( `*expr, var*` )`
Smallest coefficient of a variable	`tcoeff( `*expr, var*` )`
Degree of a polynomial	`degree( `*expr, var*` )`
Determination of the *n*th term in an expression	`op(`*n, expr*` )`
Determination of the *i*th to the *j*th term in an expression	`op(i..j, `*expr*` )`
Determination of the number of terms in an expression	`nops( `*expr*` )`
Suppression of the output	Append a colon (:) to the command

Commands for rational integral terms

2.3 Calculating with fractions (rational expressions)

The commands described in the previous section can also be used on fractions. Before we look at these, we shall first introduce the command which can be used to summarise and simplify fractions. Contrary to what might be expected from the discussion so far, this is not the `simplify` command, but the `normal` command. The `simplify` command may indeed be used on fractions, but in many cases (especially with roots in fractions) it leads to unusual outputs. Here is an example:

```
> simplify(4*(2*x+1)/sqrt(1-x)+(2*x+1)^2/(2*sqrt((1-x)^3)));
```

$$-\frac{3I(2x+1)(-3+2x)}{2(-1+x)^{3/2}}$$

```
> normal(4*(2*x+1)/sqrt(1-x)+(2*x+1)^2/(2*sqrt((1-x)^3)));
```

$$-\frac{(6x+3)(-3+2x)}{2(1-x)^{3/2}}$$

To introduce the basic commands that *Maple* has available for the manipulation of fractions, we define a variable with the name FRACTION:

```
> FRACTION:=((x-3)^2*(x+5)*(x-17))/((x-2)*(x+3)):
```

To multiply out the numerator of this fraction, we use the expand command:

```
> expand(FRACTION);
```

$$\frac{x^4}{(x-2)(x+3)} - \frac{18x^3}{(x-2)(x+3)} - \frac{4x^2}{(x-2)(x+3)} + \frac{402x}{(x-2)(x+3)} - \frac{765}{(x-2)(x+3)}$$

As can be seen, only the numerator is multiplied out and the denominator remains in the factorised form. Furthermore, the result is displayed as the sum of single fractions, in which all denominators are the same and the powers in the numerators decrease. To alter the result from the sum of single fractions, the normal command is used:

```
> normal(FRACTION);
```

$$\frac{(x-3)^2(x+5)(x-17)}{(x-2)(x+3)}$$

To be able to access the numerator and denominator of a fraction, *Maple* offers the numer and denom commands:

```
> numer(FRACTION);
```

$$(x-3)^2(x+5)(x-17)$$

```
> denom(FRACTION);
```

$$(x-2)(x+3)$$

As shown above, on multiplying out (expand) a fraction only the numerator is considered. One way of multiplying out both numerator and denominator is as follows:

```
> expand(numer(FRACTION))/expand(denom(FRACTION));
```

$$\frac{x^4-18x^3-4x^2+402x-765}{x^2+x-6}$$

To factorise the last result completely, that is, both numerator and denominator, we need the `factor` command. (Remember that the previous result is retrieved with the " sign.)

```
> factor(");
```

$$\frac{(x+5)(x-17)(x-3)^2}{(x-2)(x+3)}$$

In many applications – for example, when investigating rational terms for $x \rightarrow \pm\infty$ – one needs a way of representing a fraction that consists of a rational integral and a fractional rational term. For this, the degree of the numerator must be smaller than the degree of the denominator. This is achieved with the `convert` command, together with the `parfrac` option:

```
> convert(FRACTION,parfrac,x);
```

$$x^2 - 19x + 21 - \frac{21}{x-2} + \frac{288}{x+3}$$

To simplify terms	`normal(` *expr* `)`
To multiply out the numerator of a fraction	`expand(` *expr* `)`
To separate fractions into partial fractions	`convert(` *expr*,`parfrac`,*x* `)`
To factorise the numerator and denominator of a fraction	`factor(` *expr* `)`
Numerator of a fraction	`numer(` *expr* `)`
Denominator of a fraction	`denom(` *expr* `)`

Calculating with fractions

2.4 Problems

1. Calculate $(x + y - 17)(x^2 + 14x - 37)$.
2. Determine the coefficients of y in the term

$$(x + y - 17)(x^2 + 14x - 37).$$

3. Determine the highest power of x in the term

$$(x + y - 17)(x^2 + 14x - 37).$$

4. Calculate all linear functions of the term

$$3x^5 - 5x^4 - 27x^3 \ 45x^2 - 1200x + 2000.$$

5. Calculate

$$\frac{x^2 - 5x + 6}{x - 3}$$

6. Multiply out the numerator of the expression

$$\frac{(x - 5)(x + 14)}{(x + 11)(x - 17)}$$

7. Multiply out the numerator and denominator of the expression

$$\frac{(x - 5)(x + 14)}{(x + 11)(x - 17)}$$

8. Convert the following expression into the simplest partial fractions:

$$\frac{(x - 5)(x + 14)}{(x + 11)(x - 17)}$$

3 Lists, tables and functions

For many computer algebra packages, including *Maple*, lists are elementary data types that enable mathematical objects, such as vectors, matrices and tensors, to be represented. In everyday parlance, lists are understood to include, for example, ordered and unordered lists of names and addresses, tables, collections of dates, etc. This chapter will show the structures and commands that *Maple* offers for handling such data.

3.1 Sets

In mathematics, according to Cantor, a set is understood to be a collection of objects that we can see or imagine as a whole (ignoring a sequence, that is). The same obtains for *Maple*, including consideration of the sequence. To identify the objects that belong in a set, the objects are separated by a comma and enclosed between curly brackets. The following examples show which objects can be grouped as a set:

```
> M1:={1,2,a,b};
```

$$M1 := \{1, 2, b, a\}$$

```
> M2:={b,a,1,2};
```

$$M2 := \{1, 2, b, a\}$$

```
> M3:={a,x,y,z,17};
```

$$M3 := \{17, x, a, y, z\}$$

From the display of the sets we see that *Maple* establishes internally a sequence for the elements of a set when locating them in memory (first the numbers, then the symbols). This does not generally depend on the order of inputting the set elements. To select one element of the set ordered in this way by *Maple*, the op command may be used, as in the case of polynomials. Here is an example for the first element of set M1:

```
> op(1,M1);
```

$$1$$

Sets are compared with the 'equals' sign (=). To test whether the comparison gives a true or false result, the command evalb must be invoked; this evaluates Boolean terms. (Boolean terms are expressions that may be true or false; see chapter 8.) Such a term can be built from simpler terms by means of logical operators — and, or, etc.:

```
> evalb(M1=M2);
```

true

```
> evalb(M1=M3);
```

false

For the set operations of union, intersection and difference, there are the union, intersect and minus commands. To determine whether a symbol, number, etc., is contained in a set, in *Maple* the command member is used. The following examples illustrate the use of these commands:

```
> M1 union M3;
```

$$\{1, 2, 17, x, b, a, y, z\}$$

```
> M1 intersect M3;
```

$$\{a\}$$

```
> M1 minus M3;
```

$$\{1,2,b\}$$

```
> member(Y,M2);
```

false

The elements of a set are included within curly brackets.

Union of sets ($M1 \cup M2$)	M1 union M2
Intersection of sets ($M1 \cap M2$)	M1 intersection M2
Difference	M1 minus M2
Element of a set	member(*element, set*)
To select the *n*th element of a set	op(*n, set*)
To compare sets	evalb($M1=M2$)

Basic commands for sets

3.2   Series

The concept of series has great importance in mathematics. Here a series is understood to be a finite or an infinite sequence of numbers, in which each member, from the first and, in the case of a finite series, the last, has a unique predecessor and successor. In *Maple* there is the `seq` command to produce finite series. A term and, separated by a comma, the domain to be tabulated is passed to the command. The term can be an algebraic expression that is dependent on the table variables, or a set of such terms. (Other complex mathematical structures, such as lists, tables, etc., and their nesting can be passed to the `seq` command.) Here is an example for the squares from 1 to 10:

```
> seq(i^2,i=1..10);
```

$$1,4,9,16,25,36,49,64,81,100$$

Here we see that the table variable is always incremented by 1. Because the `seq` command has no option for the step, this must be provided by the user. One way of doing this is the next example, where the sine function from 0 to π is tabulated using the step $\pi/6$:

```
> seq(sin(Pi/6*i),i=0..6);
```

$$0,\ \frac{1}{2},\ \frac{\sqrt{3}}{2},\ 1,\ \frac{\sqrt{3}}{2},\ \frac{1}{2},\ 0$$

Another method consists of first producing a series (list; see next section) with the required step, which is then only called for the calculation of the particular series. The following example illustrates this procedure by tabulating nth roots. (Reminder: the use of the colon suppresses the output.)

```
> Series:=seq(1/i,i=1..5):
> seq(x^i,i=Series);
```

$$x,\ \sqrt{x},\sqrt[3]{x},\sqrt[4]{x},\sqrt[5]{x}$$

As mentioned above, series of sets can also be produced with the `seq` command. The result of such an operation, when enclosed within set curly brackets, produces another set. The following example shows the input for this operation:

```
> {seq({i,5-i},i=1..5)};
```

$$\{\{1,4\},\{2,3\},\{0,5\}\}$$

At first sight, one might think that something is missing here. But because the sets $\{2,3\}$ and $\{3,2\}$ as well as $\{1,4\}$ and $\{4,1\}$ are identical, only one of each is shown as element of the whole set. If we remove the set brackets from the last input, we see that all two-element sets appear.

3.3 Lists

This section discusses elementary operations with lists. *Maple* understands a list to be a collection of objects. To recognise these objects, it requires them to be separated by a comma and be enclosed between square brackets. The next examples show the kind of objects that can be collected as a list:

```
> L1:=[10,20,30];
```

$$L1 := [10,20,30]$$

```
> L2:=[a,b,x^2];
```

$$L2 := [a,b,x^2]$$

To select an element of a list, one can either use the op command or call the list name, at the same time providing the number of the required element within square brackets. Both methods are illustrated in the following examples. The second element of the first list ($L1$):

```
> op(2,L1);
```

$$20$$

```
> L1[2];
```

$$20$$

If part of a list is to be considered, then the numbers of the first and last elements, separated by two colons, together with the list name, are given to the op command. The same element input is required to call the list using square brackets. The last two elements of the second list ($L2$):

```
> op(2..3,L2);
```

$$b, x^2$$

```
> L1[2..3];
```

$$b, x^2$$

As can be seen, the result in both cases is not a list, but a series of elements. To produce a list, the selection of elements must be enclosed within square brackets. Using this method new information can be produced from the existing lists. In the next example all the elements of lists $L1$ and $L2$ are gathered together in a new list:

```
> L3:=[op(L1),op(L2)];
```

$$L3 := [10, 20, 30, a, b, x^2]$$

By using the seq command in conjunction with lists it is possible to produce very impressive tables of values. Here a list is passed to the seq command containing the tabulating variable and the tabulating term:

```
> seq([x/5,(x/5)^2],x=0..5);
```

$$[0,0],[\frac{1}{5},\frac{1}{25}],[\frac{2}{5},\frac{4}{25}],[\frac{3}{25},\frac{9}{25}],[\frac{4}{5},\frac{16}{25}],[1,1]$$

> If we want to read out a part from a list, we give the locations of the required part to the op command. If several parts are required, the op command must be called several times. In such cases the result is always given as a series and not as a list. To obtain a list, the result must be enclosed within square brackets.

The elements of a list are enclosed within square brackets.	
To select an element in the list	op (*i, list*) or *list* [*i*]
To select several elements in the list	op (*i..j, list*) or *list* [*i..j*]

Basic commands for lists

3.4 Arrays and tables

In *Maple* arrays are understood to be single- or multi-dimensional arrangements of numbers or symbols. The array command is used to produce such arrangements — for example, vectors, matrices and tensors (see chapter 5). To describe general tables, such as entries in a pocket diary, weekly stock market data, etc., the table command is used in *Maple*. The first part of this section will look at the procedure with arrays, while the second deals with general tables. First, a one-dimensional array with inputs is defined:

```
> A:=array(1..3);
```

$$A := array(1..3,[\ ])$$

This output differs from the input by the two square brackets which symbolise an empty list. (The above definition of *A* therefore corresponds to a variable declaration in a high-level language such as Pascal or C.) To fill this empty list the individual elements of the array must be assigned. So first the array name (here *A*) is called with the number of the element that is to be assigned. Then follows the value assignment with a colon and 'equals' sign (:=).

The next two examples show a value assignment for the first two elements of the array *A*:

```
> A[1]:='x';
```

$$A[1] := x$$

```
> A[2]:='y';
```

$$A[2] := y$$

In the assignment the variables are enclosed within single quotes so that the actual symbol and not an earlier value of the symbol is assigned. The previous assignments for A can be obtained with the print command:

```
> print(A);
```

$$[x,y,A[3]]$$

If an element has not been ordered, it is given the general description — here $A[3]$. If the only question to be answered is which entries are already ordered, the indices command may be used:

```
> indices(A);
```

$$[1],[2]$$

The output shows that elements 1 and 2 have been ordered. The command entries allows us to test which values were assigned:

```
> entries(A);
```

$$[x],[y]$$

In the next example a two-dimensional array is defined, consisting of three rows (first entry, the definition 1..3) and two columns (second entry, the definition 1..2). In addition, all elements of the first row are assigned as 1s and all those of the second row as 2s ([[1,1],[2,2]]):

```
> B:=array(1..3,1..2,[[1,1],[2,2]]);
```

$$B := \begin{bmatrix} 1 & 1 \\ 2 & 2 \\ ? & ? \end{bmatrix}$$

Again, with two- and multi-dimensional arrays the indices command can be used to check which elements have already been assigned. The value can be obtained with the entries command. It should be noted that the values are given in the same sequence as the assigned entries (this corresponds to the location in memory):

```
> indices(B);
```

$$[2,2],[1,2],[1,1],[2,1]$$

```
> entries(B);
```

$$[2],[1],[1],[2]$$

Because arrays are often used with specific structures, the description of these can be given as parameters to the `array` command. For null arrays there is the `sparse` option. For arrays that are symmetric to a diagonal (from top left to bottom right) there is the `symmetric` option. More detail about the parameters `antisymmetric`, `diagonal` and `identity` are given in chapter 5. Here is an example of a sparse array:

```
> C:=array(sparse,1..2,1..2);
```

$$C := array(sparse,\ 1..2,\ 1..2,\ [\ ])$$

```
> print(C);
```

$$\begin{bmatrix} 0 & 0 \\ 0 & 0 \end{bmatrix}$$

The next example describes a symmetric array in the definition of which all the elements of the first row are assigned:

```
> D:=array(symmetric,1..3,1..3,[[a,a,a]]);
```

$$D := \begin{bmatrix} a & a & a \\ a & ? & ? \\ a & ? & ? \end{bmatrix}$$

If only one element outside the diagonal is assigned, the element that lies symmetric to the diagonal receives the same value:

```
> D[2,3]:=b;
```

$$D[2,3] := b$$

```
> print(D);
```

$$\begin{bmatrix} a & a & a \\ a & ? & b \\ a & b & ? \end{bmatrix}$$

Because *Maple* recognises a great number of different list structures, there are commands for the transformation of individual structures between one another, in so far as the transformation is mathematically acceptable. To achieve this, the `convert` command is called with the object to be transformed and the target transformation. For example, all the elements of the array *D* can be converted into a set:

```
> convert(D,set);
```

$$\{b,a\}$$

Array *A* can be converted into a list:

```
> convert(A,list);
```

$$[x,y,A_3]$$

A list can be converted into an array:

```
> convert([1,2,3],array);
```

$$[1,2,3]$$

Array *D* can be converted into a list of lists:

```
> convert(D,list,list);
```

$$[[a,a,a],[a,D_{2,2},b],[a,b,D_{3,3}]]$$

The last part of this section will describe by means of an example the procedure for handling all kinds of tables in *Maple*. First the description of the table:

```
> Prime:=table([ null='Doesn't exist', first=2, second=3,
third=5]);
```

$$\text{table}([first = 2, second = 3, third = 5, null = \text{'Doesn't exist'}])$$

From the input we see that the `table` command is called with a list. If this list contains comparisons, the left side is interpreted as the index, while the right side is the content. If this list contains special structures (for example, symmetry), these can be passed as parameters, as with arrays. To select an element from a table, the table name with its index is called, the latter being enclosed within square brackets. The first prime number in the table *Prime* is thus obtained by:

```
> Prime[first];
```

Equally, new entries can be assigned or old ones described:

```
> Prime[fourth]:=7;
```

$$Prime[fourth] := 7$$

The altered table can be retrieved with the print command:

```
> print(Prime);
```

table([*first* = 2, *second* = 3, *third* = 5, *fourth* = 7, *null* 'Doesn't exist'])

To define an array	array(*option, index domain(s), list*)
To call an element of an array (table)	*name* [*index*]
To order an element of an array (table)	*name* [*index*] :=*value*
To check already-assigned entries	indices(*name*)
To check the value of already-assigned entries	entries(*name*)
To display an array (table)	print(*name*)
To produce a table	table(*option, list*)

name :name of the table or the array
index :declares the number of an entry. In multi-dimensional structures, this is a sequence of numbers, each separated by a comma
list :list with the assignment of individual elements

Commands to produce arrays and tables

3.5 Functions

In *Maple*, functions are defined in the same way as in mathematics – that is, a function can have one or several arguments, and the calculation of the function value is carried out with the aid of a value assignment. The variables of a function are named as usual in *Maple*. If several are involved, they are separated by commas. All arguments are enclosed within parentheses. (Not required for a single variable.) Assignment of the function term is by := ->. Here are some examples:

```
> f:=x->x^3;
```

$$f := x \rightarrow x^3$$

To determine the function value at a location, say 3, the function is called by its associated argument:

```
> f(3);
```

$$27$$

Now, an example for a function with two variables:

```
> g:=(x,y)->x^2+y^2;
```

$$g := (x,y) \to x^2 + y^2$$

The function value at a location is found as above:

```
> g(2,3);
```

$$13$$

We see that for x the value 2 and for y the value 3 is entered. g(x,y) is calculated with these values. If g is called with only one argument, an error message is received.

In the examples so far, only functions whose result was a real number have been illustrated. The following example shows that in *Maple* there can be functions whose result is a list perhaps:

```
> h:=(x,y,z)->[x+y,z-x];
```

$$h := (x, y, z) \to [x + y, z - x]$$

```
> h(1,5,18);
```

$$[6,17]$$

If a function is to be applied to a list or another collection of objects, this is not possible because of the strict rules for the calling of functions, namely that a function which is defined for a variable may also only be called with a variable. To be able to apply a function to several objects nevertheless, *Maple* offers the map command. The following example shows how this command can be used to apply the function f with $f(x) = x^3$ to the list L1:=[10, 20, 30] from an earlier section:

```
> map(f,L1);
```

$$[1000, 8000, 27000]$$

From the output we can see that the map command first requires the function name and then the expression on which the function is to be applied. Here an expression is understood to be a rational integral term, a list, a set, etc. The next example shows the effects on a rational integral term:

```
> map(f,a+b);
```

$$a^3 + b^3$$

Here f is applied to every object (summands) of the term.

The closing example of this section shows the production of a table of values from 0 to 3 to the example of function f:

```
> WT:=[seq([x,f(x)],x=0..3)];
```

$$[[0,0],[1,1],[2,8],[3,27]]$$

If the pairs of values are to be ordered, the list can be transformed into an array by means of the convert command:

```
> convert(WT,array);
```

$$\begin{bmatrix} 0 & 0 \\ 1 & 1 \\ 2 & 8 \\ 3 & 27 \end{bmatrix}$$

However, in *Maple* functions, or general procedures, can not only be used to realise mathematical functions, they can also be used to program. In chapter 8 a section is devoted to the technique for programming.

| Assignment of function terms | *name* =: *var* -> *term* |
| To apply a function to an expression | map (*name, expr*) |

var	:variable(s) of the function
term	:function term
expr	:expression to which the function is applied
name	:name of function

Functions

3.6   Problems

1. Define the function f with $f(x) = x \cdot \sin x$ in *Maple*.
2. Produce a table of values of function f from problem 1 from 0 to 2π with the step $\pi/6$.
3. Find with *Maple* the fifth displayed point of the table from problem 2.
4. Find with *Maple* the function value at location $\pi/2$ in the table from problem 2.

4 Solution of equations

Solving equations is an important task for algebra. One part of such tasks can be undertaken by software packages such as *Maple*. Those tasks that can, and cannot, be handled by *Maple* are described in the next section.

4.1 Solving rational integral equations

The category of rational integral equations is generally understood to include equations that only contain rational integral terms, that is, terms of the form

$$a_n x^n + a_{n-1} x^{n-1} + ... + a_0$$

which do not contain root terms, trigonometric functions, etc. By means of the following examples we shall show how *Maple* can be used to solve equations.

First, we shall determine the solution of $19x + 17 = 0$. For this *Maple* has the `solve` command:

```
> solve(19*x+17);
```

$$-\frac{17}{19}$$

From the example we see that only the term whose zero position is to be found must be given to the `solve` command. By this method of calling the equation (=0) and the solution variable are automatically determined. The next example shows the kinds of problem that may arise from such calls when solving the equation $ax - b = 0$:

```
> solve(a*x-b);
```

$$\{b = ax, x = x, a = a\}$$

The output says that the equation was solved for b and x and a were considered as free — not ordered — variables. To avoid such interpretation problems in this section, the following example describes the further call of the `solve` command. In this case, first the equation to be solved and the solution variable (separated by a comma) is given to the `solve` command. Solve the equation $ax - b = 0$ for x:

```
> solve(a*x-b=0,x);
```

38

$$\frac{b}{a}$$

The variation of the solution variables provides the corresponding solutions for *a* and *b*. The next two examples show how quadratic equations can be solved by *Maple*:

```
> solve(x^2+7*x+12=0,x);
```

$$-3, -4$$

```
> solve(5/(x-2)-3=(2*x+4)/5,x);
```

$$3, -\frac{21}{2}$$

The last example shows that solutions are always given as a series and the equations must not necessarily be input in the form *term(x)* = 0. *Maple* is also capable of solving quadratic equations with parameters:

```
> solve(2*x^2-a*x-a^2=0,x);
```

$$a, -\frac{a}{2}$$

The question now is whether such equations are solvable for every choice of parameter. *Maple* can be helpful in answering this question in that matching equations or inequalities are solved with *Maple*. However, it does not offer any command that solves this problem automatically.

The following examples show how equations of a higher degree can be solved with *Maple*:

```
> solve(14*x^3+60*x^2-246*x+140=0,x);
```

$$2, -7, \frac{5}{7}$$

```
> solve(5*x^3-3*x^2+25*x-15=0,x);
```

$$I\sqrt{5}, 3/5, -I\sqrt{5}$$

Now an example with a rather longer solution:

```
> solve(11*x^3-20*x^2-10*x+22=0,x);
```

$$\sqrt[3]{\%1} + \frac{730}{1089\sqrt[3]{\%1}} + \frac{20}{33} \, ,$$

$$-\frac{\sqrt[3]{\%1}}{2} - \frac{365}{1089\sqrt[3]{\%1}} + \frac{20}{33} + \frac{I\sqrt{3}}{2}\left(\%1 - \frac{730}{1089\sqrt[3]{\%1}}\right),$$

$$-\frac{\sqrt[3]{\%1}}{2} - \frac{365}{1089\sqrt[3]{\%1}} + \frac{20}{33} - \frac{I\sqrt{3}}{2}\left(\%1 - \frac{730}{1089\sqrt[3]{\%1}}\right),$$

$$\%1 := -\frac{18037}{35937} + \frac{I\sqrt{19493}\sqrt{3}}{1089}$$

To make the output more readable, the term(s) that is present in all solutions is replaced by %1 (generally by %number) at the outset. The value of this parameter is shown at the end of the output. I is used to describe $\sqrt{-1}$. Here a numerical approximation for these solutions can be obtained with the evalf command:

```
> evalf(");
```

$$1.613193272 + .1 * 10^{-9}\, I, \, -1.015665881, \, 1.220654427 - .2 * 10^{-9}\, I$$

Unfortunately, those values that contain an imaginary part, albeit very small, are false, because solutions are reals. The reason for this error is to be found in the internal calculating accuracy of *Maple*. If the error is caused by the default setting (10 decimal places), it must be removed by increasing the number of decimal places. Here is an attempt with 100 decimal places:

```
> Digits:=100:
> evalf(");
```

1.61319327207776985749385286563640338741749490035829978734649472926367612556959616521771724947659838 5,
−1.015665880292489575367196113353900053191396652026902785936065581158936542393475972221071453128410880 6−.1 * 10−99*I*,
4290050750748018334537517481546362569223 8−.1 * 10−99*I*

As can be seen, the error has become markedly smaller. To eliminate it completely, the calculating precision needs to be set to about 1000 decimal places. To obtain the correct numerical solutions without altering the precision, the `fsolve` command should be used. Then the problems revealed above do not arise. The syntax of this command conforms with that of the `solve` command:

```
> fsolve(11*x^3-20*x^2-10*x+22=0,x);
```

$$1.613193272, -1.015665880, 1.220654426$$

As indicated already, *Maple* can also be used to solve equations of higher degree. In general, from the theory of equations, this is only possible for equations of degree at most 4. If equations of higher degree are considered, *Maple* reaches its limits. Here are some examples:

```
> solve(19*x^9+57*x^6-3*x^5-9*x^2+323*x^7+969*x^4-51*x^3
> -153=0,x);
```

$$\sqrt{17}, \frac{\sqrt[3]{3}}{2} - \frac{13^{5/6}}{2}, \frac{\sqrt[3]{3}}{2} + \frac{13^{5/6}}{2}, -\sqrt[3]{3}, -I\sqrt{17},$$

$$-\frac{I\,19^{3/4}\sqrt[4]{3}}{19}, -\frac{19^{3/4}\sqrt[4]{3}}{19}, \frac{I\,19^{3/4}\sqrt[4]{3}}{19}, \frac{19^{3/4}\sqrt[4]{3}}{19}$$

```
> solve(x^10-45*x^9+17x^6-93*x^4+34*x-156=0,x);
```

$$RootOf(\_Z^{10} - 45\_Z^9 + 17\_Z^6 - 93\_Z^4 + 34\_Z - 156)$$

```
> fsolve(x^10-45*x^9+17*x^6-93*x^4+34*x-156=0,x,complex);
```

0.6443338901 −0.8262209069*I*, −0.3128669193 −1.226430666*I*,
1.059405142 −0.5009708716*I*, −0.7619421505 + 0.7487999050*I*,
0.6443338901 + 0.8262209069*I*, −0.3128669193 + 1.226430666*I*,
1.059405142 + 0.5009708716*I*, −0.7619421505 −0.7487999050*I*,
−1.257663869, 44.99981394

In the analytical solution of the second *Maple* can find no solution; for this reason the solution (`RootsOf`) is output symbolically, that is, not simplified, with the variables represented by `_Z`. The `fsolve` command allows all solutions to be calculated numerically, provided that it is called with the `complex` option. Otherwise only the real solutions are determined.

4.2 Equations with square roots and absolute values

Apart from purely algebraic equations, *Maple* can also solve those that can be reduced to the algebraic. Roots and absolute value equations are two representatives of this category. In this section we shall first define the equations in order to focus more easily on the parts that have to be manipulated.

Here is an example for a root equation:

```
> EQ1:= sqrt(5*x-1)=x-5;
```

$$\sqrt{5x-1} = x-5$$

Now the first attempt at a solution:

$$2,13$$

In order to obtain the correct solutions with root equations, a test must be carried out with all solutions. That is, the right and left sides of the equation must be evaluated for $x = 2$ and $x = 13$. To achieve this, there are three *Maple* commands:

1. lhs, to obtain the left-hand side
2. rhs, to obtain the right-hand side
3. subs, to substitute a variable in a term

The following inputs illustrate the application of these commands. First the test for $x = 2$:

The left side:
```
> subs(x=2,lhs(EQ1));
```

$$\sqrt{9}$$

The right side:
```
> subs(x=2,rhs(EQ1));
```

$$-3$$

Now, the test for $x = 13$:

The left side:
```
> subs(x=13,lhs(EQ1));
```

$$\sqrt{64}$$

The right side:
```
> subs(x=13,rhs(EQ1));
```

If one compares the left and right sides of both solutions, it is clear that for $x = 2$ they do not agree ($\sqrt{9} \neq -3$), but for $x = 13$ they do ($\sqrt{64} = 8$). Thus, only 13 is a solution for the equation. Unfortunately, *Maple* offers no option for a test to be carried out automatically. However, because *Maple* is freely programmable, the procedure described above can be reduced to a command (see chapter 8).

Next we consider an example for a sum equation. First the equation is ordered:

```
> EQ2:= abs(x^2-10*x+20)=4;
```

$$|x^2 - 10x + 20| = 4$$

Now the solution:

```
> solve(EQ2,x);
```

$$8, 2, 6, 4$$

All of these are solutions (see problem 5).

4.3 Trigonometric equations

Many trigonometric equations can be converted into algebraic equations, but problems often arise when a complete analytical solution is attempted. Here is a simple example:

```
> solve(sin(x)=1/2,x);
```

$$\frac{\pi}{6}$$

From the output we can see that only one solution – often called the principal value – is given, even though the equation has infinitely many solutions. Further solutions can be obtained by utilising the periodicity (2π) of the sine function. But even this does not yield all. The graphical capabilities of *Maple* allow the user to determine all the solutions by grouping the left and right sides of the equation as function terms. Both of these can be plotted as a graph (see chapter 6) from which the solutions may be read off.

We now include some more complex examples. Here, as in the first section, the equation is first assigned to a variable and then solved:

```
> EQ1:=3*tan(x)+2=cot(x);
```

$$3 \tan(x) + 2 = \cot(x)$$

```
> solve(EQ1,x);
```

$$-\frac{\pi}{4}, \arctan(1/3)$$

Once again, not all solutions are determined. Because arctan(1/3) cannot be simplified symbolically, the term remains unchanged.

```
> G12:=sin(x)=cos(x);
```

$$\sin(x) = \cos(x)$$

```
> solve(EQ2,x);
```

Maple can find no solution for this equation; therefore there is no output. One possibility for solving such equations is to transform them into algebraic equations with the aid of the trigonometric Pythagoras theorem ($\sin^2 x + \cos^2 x = 1$). This additional information leads to a substitution of a trigonometric term in equation 2. This can be done with the subs command (this method is integrated in more recent versions of *Maple* V Release 2):

```
> solve(subs(cos(x)=sqrt(1-(sin(x))^2),EQ2),x);
```

$$1/4\pi, -1/4\pi$$

As mentioned above, these solutions are also incomplete and must undergo a check that is made through the substitution of the equation into a root equation. The check shows that both values are a solution. The following example shows that the method described here also provides the solutions of more complex equations:

```
> EQ3:=12*(sin(x))^2-7*sin(x)*cos(x)=12*(cos(x))^2;
```

$$12 \sin(x)^2 - 7 \sin(x) \cos(x) = 12 \cos(x)^2$$

```
> solve(sus(cos(x)=sqrt(1-(sin(x))^2,EQ3),x);
```

$$-2 \arctan(1/3), 2 \arctan(2),$$
$$-2 \arctan(3), -2 \arctan(1/2),$$
$$2 \arctan(1/3), 2 \arctan(3),$$
$$2 \arctan(1/2), -2 \arctan(2)$$

We see that the method described above is applied successfully here. This procedure does not succeed with all problems; in this case other substitutions must be input. These can be taken from a collection of rules. Here, though, one should not conceal the fact that the search for a usable substitution can be very time consuming.

'Equals' sign for equations	=
To solve equation(s)	`solve` (*ls=rs,var*)
To solve equation(s) numerically	`fsolve` (*ls=rs,var,options*)

The `complex` option also allows `fsolve` to determine complex solutions.

Left side of an equation	`lhs` (*EQ*)
Right side of an equation	`rhs` (*EQ*)
To substitute terms	`subs` (*t1=t2,t3*)

ls   :left side of equation
rs   :right side of equation
var :solution variable
EQ   :equation
t1   :term that is substituted
t2   :term that substitutes
t3   :term in which substitution occurs

With `solve` sets of equations and solution variables can be declared (see chapter 5).

Solution of equations

4.4   Problems

1. Solve the equation $15x^2 - 2x - 8 = 0$.
2. Solve the equation $x^4 - 4x^3 = 17x^2 + 16x + 84$.
3. Solve the equation

$$\sqrt{x+2} - 1 = \sqrt{x}$$

4. Solve the equation $2\cos^2 x + 3\cos x + 1 = 0$.
5. Check all the solutions of the equation

$$|x^2 - 10x + 20| = 4$$

5 Linear algebra and systems of equations

5.1 Description of matrices and vectors

Vectors and matrices are displayed in *Maple* as arrays (see chapter 3). They can therefore be described and handled like arrays. This means that, for example, a matrix or vector entry can be ordered or modified by calling the appropriate index. Here is an example for the description of a vector with 5 entries and a 3×4 matrix:

```
> VECTOR:=array(1..5,[a,b,c,1,2]);
```

$$VECTOR:=[a,b,c,1,2]$$

First the definition of the matrix without output of the result:

```
> MATRIX:=array(1..3,1..4):
```

then the output produced with the aid of the print command:

```
> print(MATRIX);
```

$$\begin{bmatrix} MATRIX[1,1] & MATRIX[1,2] & MATRIX[1,3] & MATRIX[1,4] \\ MATRIX[2,1] & MATRIX[2,2] & MATRIX[2,3] & MATRIX[2,4] \\ MATRIX[3,1] & MATRIX[3,2] & MATRIX[3,3] & MATRIX[3,4] \end{bmatrix}$$

Often, matrices with special structures are required. To produce these the array command with options must be invoked. Normally, the following are available:

Matrix type	Option
Symmetric	symmetric
Antisymmetric	antisymmetric
Sparse	sparse
Diagonal	diagonal
Identity	identity

As we have already given examples of symmetric and sparse matrices in chapter 3, we now give examples of the other options.

An antisymmetric matrix:

```
> MA:=array(antisymmetric,1..3,1..3):
> print(MA);
```

$$\begin{bmatrix} 0 & MA[1,2] & MA[1,3] \\ -MA[1,2] & 0 & MA[2,3] \\ -MA[1,3] & -MA[2,3] & 0 \end{bmatrix}$$

As can be seen, in an antisymmetric matrix the diagonal is filled with zeros; the other elements are reflected in the diagonal, with a change of sign.

A diagonal matrix:

```
> MD:=array(diagonal,1..3,1..3):
> print(MD);
```

$$\begin{bmatrix} MD[1,1] & 0 & 0 \\ 0 & MD[2,2] & 0 \\ 0 & 0 & MD[3,3] \end{bmatrix}$$

The identity matrix:
```
> MI:=array(identity,1..3,1..3):
> print(MI);
```

$$\begin{bmatrix} 1 & 0 & 0 \\ 0 & 1 & 0 \\ 0 & 0 & 1 \end{bmatrix}$$

To describe a matrix	array(*option,1..imax,1..jmax, ord*)
To describe a vector	array(*1..imax*)
Element of a matrix	*m* [*i,j*]
Diagonal matrix	array(*diagonal,1..imax,1..jmax*)
Identity matrix	array(*identity,1..imax,1..jmax*)

m	:matrix
i	:row number
j	:column number
imax	:maximum row number
jmax	:maximum column number
ord	:list of ordered elements

Matrices

5.2 Calculating with vectors

The description of vectors in the previous section can be used provided that no supplementary commands are called. However, for example, in order to calculate the vector products, these must be loaded. In this section, to avoid operating with two definitions for the same vectors, first we shall outline how new commands are loaded and then define the vectors for further work.

Supplementary commands (packages) are loaded by the *Maple* command with. As this section will describe some phenomena from linear algebra, the linalg package is loaded. The form of the call is as follows:

```
> with(linalg);
Warning: new definition for    norm
Warning: new definition for    trace

[BlockDiagonal, GramSchmidt, JordanBlock, Wronskian, add,
addcol, addrow, adj, adjoint, angle, augment, backsub,
band, basis, bezout, blockmatrix, charmat, charpoly, col,
coldim, colspace, colspan, companion, concat, cond,
copyinto, crossprod, curl, definite, delcols, delrows, det,
diag, diverge, dotprod, eigenvals, eigenvects, entermatrix,
equal, exponential, extend, ffgausselim, fibonacci,
frobenius, gausselim, gaussjord, genmatrix, grad, hadamard,
hermite, hessian, hilbert, htranspose, ihermite, indexfunc,
innerprod, intbasis, inverse, ismith, iszero, jacobian,
jordan, kernel, laplacian, leastsqrs, linsolve, matrix,
minor, minpoly, mulcol, mulrow, multiply, norm, normalize,
nullspace, orthog, permanent, pivot, potential, randmatrix,
randvector, range, rank, ratform, row, rowdim, rowspace,
rowspan, rref, scalarmul, singularvals, smith, stack,
submatrix, subvector, sumbasis, swapcol, swaprow,
sylvester, toeplitz, trace, transpose, vandermonde,
vecpotent, vectdim, vector]
```

After two warning messages about the alteration of the norm and trace commands, there follows a list of the commands that can be used after loading of the package.

In what follows, three vectors will be assigned with the new vector command (see above). For this the command is called with either a list or a numeral that assigns the number of the entry (dimension). In the second kind of call all entries (coordinates) are free, that is, any desired numbers or symbols can be assigned. The assignment is:

```
> VECTOR1:=vector(3):
> print(VECTOR1);
```

$$[VECTOR1[1], VECTOR1[2], VECTOR1[3]]$$

```
> VECTOR2:=vector(3):
> print(VECTOR2);
```

$$[VECTOR2[1], VECTOR2[2], VECTOR2[3]]$$

```
> VECTOR3:=vector(2):
> print(VECTOR3);
```

$$[VECTOR3[1], VECTOR3[2]]$$

The sum of the first pair of vectors:
```
> VECTOR1+VECTOR2;
```

$$VECTOR1 + VECTOR2$$

Here, as with complex numbers, the output only provides the formatted input, without carrying out a calculation. To achieve this, a command must be used to evaluate the term. For vectors and matrices the command is `evalm`:

```
> evalm(");
```

$$[VECTOR1[1] + VECTOR2[1],$$
$$VECTOR1[2] + VECTOR2[2],$$
$$VECTOR1[3] + VECTOR2[3]]$$

In the next example an attempt is made to subtract the second and third vectors:

```
> evalm(VECTOR2-VECTOR3);
Error, (in linalg[add]) vector dimensions incompatible
```

Because the vectors do not have the same dimension (number of entries), *Maple* refuses to carry out the subtraction and displays an error message stating that the dimensions are incompatible. The following example shows the multiplication of a vector by a number (scalar multiplication):

```
> evalm(5*VECTOR1);
```

$$[5VECTOR1[1], 5VECTOR1[2], 5VECTOR1[3]]$$

Up to this example all transformations are possible with the definitions for vectors given in the previous section. For the scalar product of two vectors a new command (`dotprod`) is required; this is contained in the `linalg` package.
The scalar product of the first pair of vectors:

```
> dotprod(VECTOR1 , VECTOR2);
```

$$VECTOR1[1]VECTOR2[1] + VECTOR1[2]VECTOR2[2] +$$
$$VECTOR1[3]VECTOR2[3]$$

Here the scalar product is calculated in the usual way. But attempting to calculate the scalar product of the last pair of vectors provokes an error message, as in the case of subtraction:

```
>dotprod(VECTOR2 , VECTOR3);
Error, (in dotprod) arguments not compatible
```

When calculating with vectors, the cross product of two vectors is often needed. In *Maple* the `crossprod` command from `linalg` is used.

We now give two examples for calculating the cross product; first a simple example, then the cross product of the vectors VECTOR1 and VECTOR2:

```
> crossprod(vector([1,0,0]),vector([0,1,0]));
```

$$[0,0,1]$$

```
> crossprod(VECTOR1 , VECTOR2);
```

$$[VECTOR1[2]VECTOR2[3] - VECTOR1[3]VECTOR2[2],$$
$$VECTOR1[3]VECTOR2[1] - VECTOR1[1]VECTOR2[3],$$
$$VECTOR1[1]VECTOR2[2] - VECTOR1[2]VECTOR2[1]]$$

In the first of the above examples we see that only vectors are given to the crossprod command, not lists. This can happen as above by passing the list to the vector command. Another possibility is to transform the list into a vector with the aid of the convert (*list*, vector) command. As with all the other linalg commands, care is needed if the commands expect vectors; otherwise error messages appear.

To define a vector	vector(n) or vector(*list*)
To add vectors	evalm($v1 + v2$)
To multiply a vector by a number	evalm($t * v1$)
Scalar product	dotprod($v1, v2$)
Cross product	crossprod($v1, v2$)
To convert a list into a vector	convert(*list*, vector)
n :natural number (dimension)	
$v1,v2$:vectors	
t :number	

Calculating with vectors

5.3   Matrix transformations

As described above, in *Maple* matrices can be regarded as two-dimensional arrays. As in the case of vectors, basic manipulations with this description are also possible for matrices. Because the linear algebra package (linalg) contains a great number of useful commands, the matrices for further work are defined in such a way that all commands in the package can be applied. Those transformations that are also possible without the package are noted in the text. It is not possible to describe here all the commands in the linalg package, which occupy more than 50 pages of the large-format manual. However, the selection given should cover the most frequently required transformations for matrices.

First, the linalg package is loaded, and three matrices are defined with the `matrix` command. To suppress the output from the `linalg` commands, the load command is terminated with a colon:

```
> with(linalg);
Warning: new definition for    norm
Warning: new definition for    trace

> matrix1:=MATRIX(3,3, [1,2,3,4,5,6,7,8,9]);
```

$$MATRIX1 \begin{bmatrix} 1 & 2 & 3 \\ 4 & 5 & 6 \\ 7 & 8 & 9 \end{bmatrix}$$

```
> MATRIX2:=matrix(3,3 [11,12,13,14,15,16,17,18,19]);
```

$$MATRIX2 \begin{bmatrix} 11 & 12 & 13 \\ 14 & 15 & 16 \\ 17 & 18 & 19 \end{bmatrix}$$

```
> MATRIX3:=matrix(2,3, [21,22,23,24,25,26]);
```

$$MATRIX3 \begin{bmatrix} 21 & 22 & 23 \\ 24 & 25 & 26 \end{bmatrix}$$

The `matrix` command is first called with the number of rows, then the columns and optionally with a value assignment of the matrix elements. To solve parts of a matrix, the domain of the appropriate rows and columns is given to the `submatrix` command. In the next example the second and third rows and the second and third columns of the second matrix are extracted:

```
> submatrix(MATRIX2,2..3,2..3);
```

$$\begin{bmatrix} 15 & 16 \\ 18 & 19 \end{bmatrix}$$

The next two examples show how rows (`row`) and columns (`col`) of a matrix can be selected.

The second row of the first matrix:

```
> row(MATRIX1,2);
```

$$[4,5,6]$$

The third column of the first matrix:

```
> col(MATRIX1,3);
```

$$[3,6,9]$$

The results of the commands row and col are interpreted by *Maple* vectors. Because the next commands change the values of the matrix elements, the results are assigned to other variables in order to obtain the original values. Because the following commands are assigned to rows as well as columns, only one transformation is given in each case. The alternative for rows or columns is obtained by altering the end of the command. The commands for rows always terminate with row and those for columns with the ending col.

To swap rows the swaprow command is used. To swap the third and second rows of the second matrix:

```
> MATRIX4:=swaprow(MATRIX2,3,2);
```

$$\begin{bmatrix} 11 & 12 & 13 \\ 17 & 18 & 19 \\ 14 & 15 & 16 \end{bmatrix}$$

The addrow command is available to add rows. A factor, and the rows to be added, are given to this command. The rows called are multiplied by this factor. If the factor is not provided at the call, it has the default value of 1. The result is displayed in the row that is invoked in the second location.

In the addition of the first and second rows of the third matrix the multiplier is chosen such that the new matrix contains a zero at the location [2,3]:

```
> MATRIX5:=addrow(MATRIX3,1,2,-MATRIX3[2,3]/MATRIX3[1,3]);
```

$$\begin{bmatrix} 21 & 22 & 23 \\ \frac{6}{23} & \frac{3}{23} & 0 \end{bmatrix}$$

To multiply a column of a matrix by a number the name of the matrix, the column number and the multiplier are passed to the mulcol command:

```
> MATRIX6:=mulcol(MATRIX1,1,41);
```

$$\begin{bmatrix} 41 & 2 & 3 \\ 164 & 5 & 6 \\ 287 & 8 & 9 \end{bmatrix}$$

To delete a row or several rows from a matrix, the name and the domain of the rows to be deleted are passed to the delrows command:

```
> MATRIX7:=delrows(MATRIX2,1..2);
```

$$[\ 17\quad 18\quad 19\ ]$$

In many cases a new matrix has to be constructed from existing ones. The stack command is used to create a new set of rows, while the concat command places the columns together one after another. The augment command can also be used as an alternative to concat. In every case the matrices are given to the commands in the order in which they are to be arranged:

```
> stack(MATRIX1,MATRIX3);
```

$$\begin{bmatrix} 1 & 2 & 3 \\ 4 & 5 & 6 \\ 7 & 8 & 9 \\ 21 & 22 & 23 \\ 24 & 25 & 26 \end{bmatrix}$$

```
>concat(MATRIX1,MATRIX2);
```

$$\begin{bmatrix} 1 & 2 & 3 & 11 & 12 & 13 \\ 4 & 5 & 6 & 14 & 15 & 16 \\ 7 & 8 & 9 & 17 & 18 & 19 \end{bmatrix}$$

In many cases it is an advantage to copy parts of one matrix into another. To achieve this, the matrix to be copied, the target matrix and the upper left location in the target matrix into which the block is to be written, are all passed to the copyinto command. If the block to be copied is too large, the oversize elements are truncated:

```
> MATRIX8:=copyinto(MATRIX1,MATRIX3,1,2);
```

$$\begin{bmatrix} 21 & 1 & 2 \\ 24 & 4 & 5 \end{bmatrix}$$

Up to this point, all the commands for matrices have come from the `linalg` package. The following commands for the addition and multiplication of matrices can also be used without resorting to that package. The sum of the first two matrices:

```
> MATRIX1+MATRIX2;
```

$$MATRIX1 + MATRIX2$$

Here *Maple* only displays the input. We have already met this with complex numbers and vectors, where the result had to be evaluated. The command to evaluate matrices is `evalm`:

```
> evalm(");
```

$$\begin{bmatrix} 12 & 14 & 16 \\ 18 & 20 & 22 \\ 24 & 26 & 28 \end{bmatrix}$$

Now, we attempt to add the first and the third matrices:

```
> evalm(MATRIX1+MATRIX3);
Error, (in linalg[add]) matrix dimensions incompatible
```

The output shows that the addition cannot take place because of different dimensions. Here *Maple* behaves according to the usual mathematical rules, as it does with all other matrix transformations.

To distinguish matrix multiplication from the multiplication of numbers, an ampersand (&) is placed in front of the multiplication symbol. As with addition, the result must be evaluated with `evalm`:

```
> evalm(MATRIX1 &* MATRIX2);
```

$$\begin{bmatrix} 90 & 96 & 102 \\ 216 & 231 & 246 \\ 342 & 366 & 390 \end{bmatrix}$$

The next commands to be described are once again taken from the `linalg` package. First, we attempt to obtain the inverse of the first matrix with the inverse command:

```
> inverse(MATRIX);
Error, (in inverse) singular matrix
```

The error message indicates that the first matrix is singular, that is, in at least one row nothing but zeros can be produced by elementary operations; therefore, the inversion is not possible. Because both other matrices are also singular, a new square, non-singular 2 × 2, matrix is defined:

```
> MATRIX10:=matrix(2,2,[1,2,3,4]):
```

The inverse of this matrix:

```
> inverse(MATRIX10);
```

$$\begin{bmatrix} -2 & 1 \\ 3/2 & -1/2 \end{bmatrix}$$

Now, the test:

```
> evalm(" &* MATRIX10);
```

$$\begin{bmatrix} 1 & 0 \\ 0 & 1 \end{bmatrix}$$

It is clear that the product of the inverse with the original matrix yields the entity matrix.

Next, we illustrate the transposition of matrices by means of the `transpose` command:

```
> transpose(MATRIX1);
```

$$\begin{bmatrix} 1 & 4 & 7 \\ 2 & 5 & 8 \\ 3 & 6 & 9 \end{bmatrix}$$

Since only non-singular matrices have non-zero determinant, the tenth matrix illustrates the det command. The same example shows how eigenvalues (eigenvals) can be obtained with *Maple*:

```
> det(MATRIX10);
```

$$-2$$

```
> eigenvals(MATRIX10);
```

$$\frac{5}{2} + \frac{\sqrt{33}}{2}, \frac{5}{2} - \frac{\sqrt{33}}{2}$$

To solve linear systems of equations, the Gauss method is often used, also known as Gaussian elimination. Here, *Maple* has the gausselim command to offer:

```
> gausselim(MATRIX1);
```

$$\begin{bmatrix} 1 & 2 & 3 \\ 0 & -3 & -6 \\ 0 & 0 & 0 \end{bmatrix}$$

From this example we can see that with the Gauss method rows (columns) of a matrix are converted by row addition (column addition) until there are only zeros under the main diagonal of the matrix. The following section examines the handling of systems of equations in detail.

Row of a matrix	`row` (*A,z*)
Column of a matrix	`col` (*A,s*)
Part matrix of a matrix	`submatrix` (*A,z1..z2,s1..s2*)
To swap two rows	`swaprow` (*A,z1,z2*)
To swap two columns	`swapcol` (*A,s1,s2*)
Addition of two rows	`addrow` (*A,z1,z2,factor*)
Addition of two columns	`addcol` (*A,s1,s2,factor*)
To delete rows	`delrows` (*A,z1..z2*)
To delete columns	`delcols` (*A,s1..s2*)
Multiplication of a row by a term	`mulrow` (*A,z,term*)
Multiplication of a column by a term	`mulcol` (*A,s,term*)
To join matrices as rows	`stack` (*A,B*)
To join matrices as columns	`concat` (*A,B*)
	`augment` (*A,B*)
To copy parts of one matrix into another	`copyinto` (*A,B,m,n*)
Matrix addition	`evalm`(*A + B*)
Matrix multiplication	`evalm`(*A* &* *B*)
Matrix inversion for square matrices	`inverse`(*A*) or
	`evalm`(*A^*(-1))
Transposed values of a matrix	`transpose`(*A*)
Eigenvalues of a square matrix	`eigenvals`(*A*)
Determinants of a square matrix	`det`(*A*)
Gaussian methods for a matrix	`gausselim`(*A*)

A, B	:	matrices
z, z1, z2	:	row numbers
s, s1, s2	:	column numbers
m, nm	:	row, column numbers of the location of the target matrix into which a matrix is to be copied

Calculating with matrices

5.4   Solution of systems of equations

First, we shall examine linear systems of equations in more depth, so that the solution of any system of equations can be illustrated by means of examples.

Just as with equations, *Maple* allows the command `solve` to be used for solving linear systems of equations. The only question is the method of input of the equation system. A simple possibility is to input the equations and solution variables as sets. The exact form of the input can be seen from the following example:

```
> solve({x+y+z=1,2*x+y+z=3,x-y+2*z=0},{x,y,z});
```

$$\{y = 0, z = -1, x = 2\}$$

Of course, *Maple* can also solve systems of equations in which the numbers of equations and variables do not agree. Here are two examples:

```
> solve({5*x+2*y=5,3*x-y=14,2*x+3*y=-9},{x,y});
```

$$\{y = -5, x = 3\}$$

```
> solve({a+b+c=3,b+c+d=1,c+d+e=-3},{a,b,c,d,e});
```

$$\{c = -b - d + 1, e = b - 4, a = d + 2, d = d, b = b\}$$

From the equations $b = b$ and $d = d$ we can see that b and d were chosen as parameters of the solution, which is logical given the structure of the solution set. If other values are chosen as parameters, these will not be invoked in the description of the solution variables. Here is an example for the parametrisation of the solutions of the last example with variables d and e:

```
> solve({a+b+c=3,b+c+d=1,c+d+e=-3},{a,b,c});
```

$$\{a = d + 2, b = 4 + e, c = -3 - e - d\}$$

In systems of equations with parameters that do not necessarily appear as linear terms, *Maple* can find the solutions, though the solution variables must be specified exactly:

```
> solve({x+a^2*z=4,y-z=0,a^2*x+y=3},{x,y,z});
```

$$\left\{x = \frac{3a^2 - 4}{-1 + a^4}, z = \frac{4a^2 - 3}{-1 + a^4}, y = \frac{4a^2 - 3}{-1 + a^4}\right\}$$

The last example shows that *Maple* also determines the solution in this case. However, it does not investigate the existence of a solution for all parameter values. Because this task, as explained to me by one of the program authors, is very difficult to program for all possible cases, there is to date no command for this purpose.

The efficiency of the `solve` command shows itself in systems of equations, which place high demands on precision in calculation. For normal-sized systems of equations *Maple* finds the exact solution (see [5]), so that it is only necessary to settle for approximate methods in the case of very large systems of equations:

```
> solve({3*x+4*y=7,300000*x+400001*y=700001},{x,y});
```

$$\{y = 1, x = 1\}$$

Maple can solve larger systems of equations, however. Because in such cases the input in the form of equations is tedious, the `linalg` package provides supplementary commands for linear systems of equations. Here, for reasons of clarity, we first define a coefficient matrix (A) and a result vector (B):

```
> with(linalg):
Warning: new definition for     norm
Warning: new definition for     trace

> A:=array([[2,1,4,-1],[1,-1,1,2],[3,0,-1,1],[4,-2,3,1]]);
```

$$\begin{bmatrix} 2 & 1 & 4 & -1 \\ 1 & -1 & 1 & 2 \\ 3 & 0 & -1 & 1 \\ 4 & -2 & 3 & 1 \end{bmatrix}$$

```
> V:=array([5,-3,2,-1]);
```

$$[5,-3, 2,-1]$$

To maintain greater clarity the coefficient matrix and the solution vector are defined as arrays, because the linsolve command, which is used to solve such equations in *Maple*, accepts this definition. Of course, the coefficient matrix can be assigned as a matrix (matrix) and the solution vector as a vector (vector). In the following call of the linsolve command the equation $A\vec{x} = V$ is solved and the solution vector $\vec{x}$ is output:

```
> linsolve(A,Y);
```

$$[1,2,0,-1]$$

The next example shows what happens when the solution contains parameters:

```
> A:=array([[2,2,-4,5],[0,0,2,-1],[1,1,1,1]]);
```

$$\begin{bmatrix} 2 & 2 & -4 & 5 \\ 0 & 0 & 2 & -1 \\ 1 & 1 & 1 & 1 \end{bmatrix}$$

```
> V:=array([5,1,4]);
```

$$[5,1,4]$$

```
> linsolve(A,V):
```

$$[-\_t_1 -3\_t_2 + 5, \_t_1, \_t_2, 2\_t_2 -1]$$

As can be seen, the parameters are numbered with t_1, t_2.... Now follow two more examples of non-linear systems of equations. These are solved with the solve command. Thus for this it is not necessary to load the `linalg` package:

```
> solve({3*x^2+4*y^2=16,4*x^2+3*y^2=19},{x,y});
```

$$\{x = 2, y = -1\}, \{x = -2, y = -1\}, \{y = 1, x = -2\}, \{y = 1, x = 2\}$$

```
> solve({x^2+y^2-18*x-18*y=-112,
>           1/2*x^2+1/2*y^2-11*x+5*y=52},{x,y});
```

$$\{\{y = 8, x = 2\}, \{y = 10, x = 16\}\}$$

From these examples it can be seen that *Maple* is well able to solve smaller non-linear equation systems. As larger systems cannot generally be solved analytically, we have to use numerical methods for their solution, as offered by the `fsolve` command.

To solve a system of equations	`solve( { `*ls* `=`*rs*`...},`*var* ` )`
To solve a linear system of equations	`linsolve(`*matrix, vector*`)`

ls	:left side of the equation
rs	:right side of the equation
var	:set with solution variables
matrix	:coefficient matrix of the system of equations
vector	:target vector of the system of equations

Solution of systems of equations

5.5 Problems

Given the following matrices:

$$M_1 = \begin{pmatrix} 1 & 2 & 3 \\ 4 & 5 & 6 \\ 7 & 8 & 9 \end{pmatrix} \quad M_2 = \begin{pmatrix} 1 & 0 & 1 \\ 0 & 1 & 0 \\ 0 & 1 & 1 \end{pmatrix}$$

1. Find the sums of the matrices M_1 and M_2.
2. Find the product of the matrices M_1 and M_2.
3. Find the transpose of the matrix M_1.
4. Calculate the determinant of the matrix M_2.
5. Calculate the inverse of the matrix M_2.
6. Solve the following system of equations:

$$\begin{aligned} 2x + 8y + 14z &= 178 \\ 7x + y + 4z &= 74 \\ 4x + 7y + 24z &= 77 \end{aligned}$$

6 Graphics

A powerful feature of *Maple* is its generation of diagrams. It is especially attractive in its most recent version (*Maple* V Release 2) for its ability to produce three-dimensional displays.

In this chapter we examine first two-dimensional graphics, followed by three-dimensional graphics.

6.1   2D-graphics

The powerful `plot` command is used to draw the graph of a function with *Maple*. The reason for the description 'powerful' is because some parameters can be given to it and a large number of options can be applied. A complete description of all these options is beyond the scope of this book, so we shall only describe some of the important ones. The object to be drawn, usually a function, is simply given to the `plot` command. If the plot area for the x-value is not given, many versions default to -10 to 10. The range for the y-value, if not given as third argument, is automatically determined. The following example illustrates the graph of the sine function:

```
> plot(sin(x),x=-Pi..Pi);
```

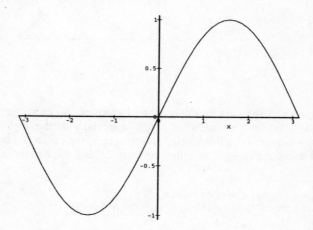

If the diagrams of several functions are to be displayed in a coordinate system, the functions are given to the `plot` command as a set, enclosed within curly brackets:

```
> plot({sin(x),sin(5*)},x=-Pi..Pi);
```

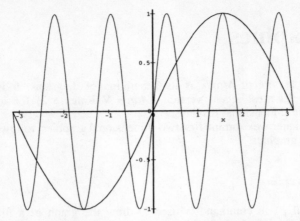

In these two examples the outputs of the graphs are formatted to optimise use of the plotting domain. For this reason the axes have different scales. By setting the `scaling` option to the value CONSTRAINED somewhat similar lengths can be achieved. The default value of the `scaling` option is UNCONSTRAINED. The previous example may be replotted with the same scale on both axes by making the following call to the `plot` command:

```
> plot({sin(x),sin(5*x)},x=Pi..Pi,scaling=CONSTRAINED);
```

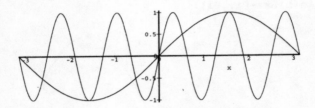

The displays of the sine function in the examples shown so far appear, on the screen at least, to be somewhat rough, especially at the high points. By increasing the number of points plotted (`numpoints`) the curve can be smoothed (the default value for `numpoints` lies between 25 and 49, depending upon the computer):

```
> plot({sin(x),sin(5*x)},x=-Pi..Pi,
        scaling=CONSTRAINED,numpoints=1000);
```

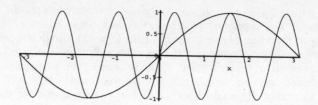

The axes option allows the axes to be positioned. With FRAME they are drawn to the left side and underside; BOXED encloses the graph in a complete frame:

```
> plot({sin(x),sin(5*x)},x=-Pi..Pi,axes=FRAME);
```

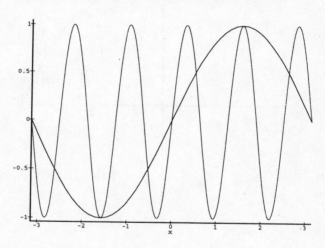

```
> plot({sin(x),sin(5*x)},x=-Pi..Pi,axes=BOXED);
```

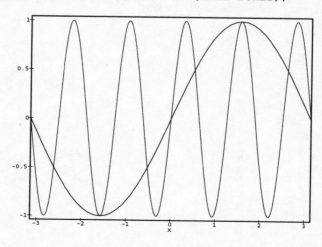

The usual setting for axes is NORMAL; the value NONE prevents the axes from being drawn. The options xtickmarks and ytickmarks control the subdividing of the axes. *Maple* generally tries to select a logical graduation for the axes automatically; however, if this does not meet the user's needs, a number greater than 1 is assigned to xtickmarks or ytickmarks. These numbers should not be too large, though, otherwise they will overwrite neighbouring marks. Here is a finer subdivision of the *x*-axis for the previous examples:

```
> plot({sin(x),sin(5*)},x=-Pi..Pi,xtickmarks=10);
```

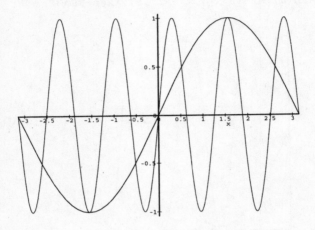

The title option is used to provide a graph with a caption. The required description is enclosed within single quotes:

```
> plot({sin(x),sin(5*x)},x=-Pi..Pi,title='sin(x),sin(5x)');
```

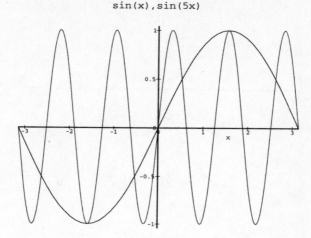

sin(x),sin(5x)

On the screen display, graphs can be distinguished by colour using the `color` option. As this cannot be shown here, we shall use another method of differentiation. This will require other commands, contained in the auxiliary package `plots`, which must first be loaded:

```
> with(plots);
[animate, animate3d, conformal, contourplot, cylinderplot,
densityplot,  display,  display3d,  fieldplot,  fieldplot3d,
gradplot,    gradplot3d,    implicitplot,    implicitplot3d,
loglogplot,   logplot,   matrixplot,   odeplot,   pointplot,
polarplot, polygonplot, polygonplot3d, polyhedraplot, replot,
setoptions,   setoptions3d,   spacecurve,   sparsematrixplot,
sphereplot, surfdata, textplot, textplot3d, tubeplot]
```

The `style` option allows the form of the line to be altered by the values POINT, LINE and PATCH. The default setting is LINE. Taking the previous example, if the first curve ($\sin(x)$) is plotted in the default mode and the second ($\sin(5x)$) as a sequence of points, both graphs are more easily distinguished. First, both graphs are plotted, but the output is suppressed:

```
> B1:=plot(sin(x),x=-Pi..Pi):
> B2:=plot(sin(5*x),x=-Pi..Pi,style=POINT):
```

Both graphs can be plotted in a coordinate system with the command `display` from the `plots` package. To achieve this the names of the graphs must be enclosed within curly brackets:

```
> display({B1,B2});
```

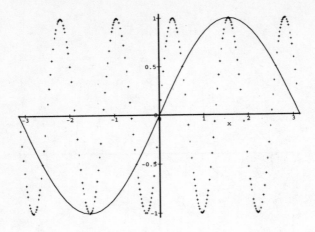

6.1.1 *Parametrised curves*

Many applications involve parametrised curves. The same command `plot` is available to draw these curves. Both the parametrised curves and the scope of the parameters are passed to the `plot` command within square brackets. The first example shows a logarithmic spiral:

```
> plot([t/5*cos(t),t/5*sin(t),t=0..10*Pi]);
```

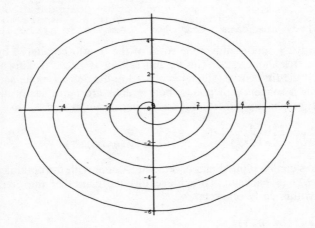

If several curves are to be shown in a graph, the following procedure is used:

- Enclose description of curves with parameters in square brackets
- Separate descriptions by commas
- Give everything to the `plot` command enclosed within curly brackets

The following example describes three concentric circles:

```
> plot({[cos(t),sin(t),t=0..2*Pi],
>       [2*cos(t),2*sin(t),t=0..2*Pi],
>       [3*cos(t),3*sin(t),t=0..2*Pi]});
```

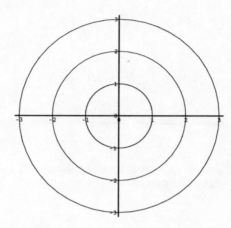

Of course, different graphs can be brought together into one, using the `display` command described in the previous section.

It should also be mentioned here that the `polarplot` command from the `plots` package enables parametrised curves to be plotted more easily. Thus calling `polarplot(1)` produces the plot of a circle with radius 1.

6.1.2 Representation of tables

An application that often arises is the graphical representation of tables. To explain the procedure, we shall first define a table. Since Release 2 of *Maple* V, tables can also be read in from a data carrier with aid of the `readdata` command. The only important requirement is for each entry to consist of exactly two plottable numbers, that is, the list must contain no symbols that *Maple* cannot convert into decimal numbers:

```
> TABLE:=[[0,0],[1,1],[2,0],[3,1],[4,0]:
```

The values of the table can be put into a graph with the `plot` command:

```
> plot(TABLE);
```

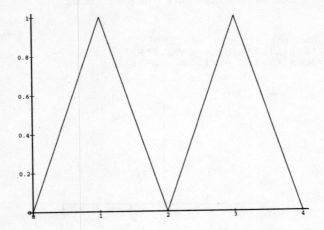

As can be seen, the points are joined; by using the POINT option of the `style` command only the points are plotted.

To plot the graph of a function	`plot({ `*sequence*` },`
	var=varmin..varmax,options `)`
To plot parametrised curves	`plot({[`*x(t),y(t),t=tmin..tmax*`]}`
	var=varmin..varmax,options`)`
To plot tables	`plot([[`x_1,y_1`],[`x_2,y_2`]...]`
	var=varmin..varmax,options`)`
To set the plot style	`style=`
	`POINT` only plot points
	`LINE` join points by a curve (default)
	`PATCH` join points by a straight line
To label drawings	`title='text'`
To determine location of	`axes=`
coordinate system	`NORMAL` in the graph (default)
	`FRAME` at the left lower border
	`BOXED` at the left lower border with frame
	`NONE` no axes
To alter the axes calibration	`xtickmarks` = *n* for *x*-axis
	`ytickmarks` = *n* for *y*-axis
To alter scaling of axes	`scaling =`
	`CONSTRAINED` same scale on both axes
	`UNCONSTRAINED` different scale on both axes (default)
To fix number of plot points	`numpoints` = *n* (default is 25 to 49)
To display graphic	`display(`*graphic*`)` (`plots` must be loaded for this)

The values of options must be either all in lower case or all in upper case.

sequence	:sequence of functions
var	:variable descriptor
varmin	:smallest value for the variable
varmax	:largest value for the variable
t	:parameter
tmin	:smallest value for the parameter
tmax	:largest value for the parameter
x_1,y_1...	:decimal numbers
n	:integer greater than 1
graphic	:set, consisting of graphics elements

2-D graphics

6.2   3D-graphics

This section describes the plot3d command which is required to draw three-dimensional graphics. For reasons of space we shall not go into all the commands of the plots package. The syntax of plot3d corresponds to the plot command in the plane in that here only a function — and not a set of functions — can be represented. Similarly, plot3d possesses a large number of options that are compatible with those of plot and in some cases gain enhancements. A selection of these will be presented in what follows.

The plot3d command requires to have given to it a function term with two variables as well as the domains of both variables:

```
> plot3d(x^2-y^2,x=-3..3,y=-3..3);
```

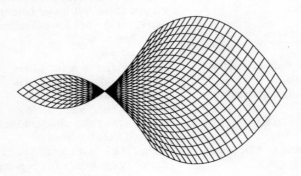

As can be seen, the function is displayed as a wire frame model without axes. Using the axes option set at NORMAL instead of the default setting NONE, the coordinate system is introduced into the graph (as below):

```
> plot3d(x^2-y^2,x=-3..3,y=-3..3,axes=NORMAL);
```

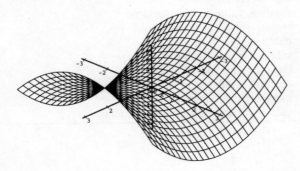

If we wish to view the graph from a different viewpoint, this can be achieved with the orientation option. The two angle coordinates of the viewing direction are given in degrees, enclosed between square brackets; default values for both are 45°. In the next example the previous example is viewed from the direction of the *y*-axis:

```
> plot3d(x^2-y^2,x=-3..3,
y=-3..3,axes=NORMAL,orientation=[90,90]);
```

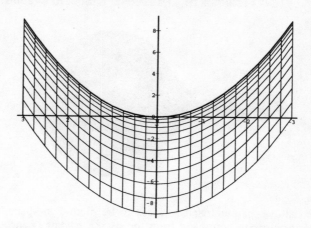

If the plotted lines appear too uneven, the number of plot points can be increased. The penalty is of course more use of memory and a delay; however, the results often repay the waiting. The next example shows the effect of plotting 50 (instead of 25) points per line. numpoints always expects the square of the number of points per line to be input. In addition, by setting the style option to PATCH the surface can be filled:

```
> plot3d(x^2-y^2,x=-3..3,y=-3..3,axes=NORMAL,
        style=PATCH,numpoints=2500);
```

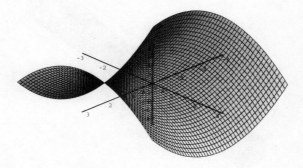

Here, the connecting lines appear much softer. However, too many lines in a drawing can be disturbing. In this case, the style option can be set to PATCHNOGRID in order to suppress the display of the lattice lines. By changing the shading option to the z value, the colour scale (grey scale) can be altered from blue to red for increasing values of *z*. The default value is system dependent, so that not all values (for example, ZHUE) are available on all systems. The next example shows the effect of both options:

```
> plot3d(x^2-y^2,x=-3..3,y=-3..3,axes=NORMAL,
          style=PATCHNOGRID,shading=Z,numpoints=2500);
```

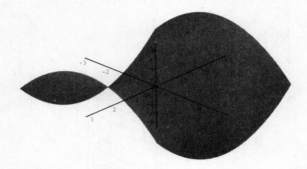

plot3d also allows parametrised surfaces to be plotted in space. (For space curves the spacecurve command from the plots package can be used.) As with the plot command, the plot3d command is given a list that here contains the parametrised *x*, *y* and *z* values of the surface. The domains of the parameters are finally given, separated by commas. In the next two examples the command is used to plot a cylinder and a torus:

```
> plot3d([t,cos(u),sin(u)],t=-8..8,u=0..2*Pi,axes=BOXED,
>         scaling=CONSTRAINED,style=PATCH,shading=Z);
```

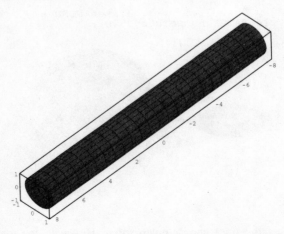

```
> plot3d([(5+cos(u))*cos(t),(5+cos(u))*sin(t),sin(u)],
>        t=0..2*Pi,u=0..2*Pi,axes=BOXED,
>        scaling=CONSTRAINED,style=PATCH,shading=Z);
```

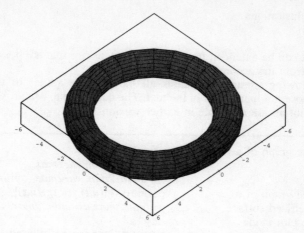

In both cases the same units were chosen for all axes (scaling+CONSTRAINED). To plot the last two graphics in a single display, the display3d command from the plots package can be used; this must be loaded by the with(plots); command. The other method is to call the command in the following form:

```
> plots[display3d]({"",""});
```

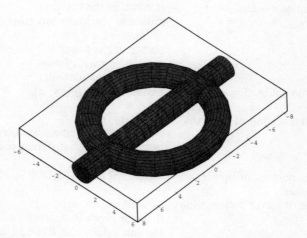

Here, first the name of the package and then the name of the command in square brackets is input. Apart from this, the syntax of the command used should be observed.

The examples presented here reveal only a small sample of the graphical capabilities of *Maple*. Other application areas are:

- List graphics
- Uniform illustrations
- Animation

These tables can be extended further. Those extensions that are possible can be discovered from the accompanying packages.

The following summary contains all the possible values of the options, including those not mentioned in the text. The data refer to *Maple* V Release 2. Therefore, not all are available in earlier versions.

To plot the graph of a function	`plot3D` (*term, var1=var1min..var1max, var2=var2min..var2max, options*)
To plot the graph of a parametrised surface	`plot3d` ([*x(u,t),y(u,t),z(u,t)*], ,*t=tmin..tmax,u=umin..umax, options*)
To set the plot mode	`style=`
	`HIDDEN` lines are not plotted (default)
	`PATCH` fill surfaces with polygons
	`PATCHNOGRID` wire frame not plotted, only the polygons
	Other options are: `POINT`, `WIREFRAME`, `CONTOUR`, `PATCHCONTOUR`, `LINE`
To title a graph	`title='text'`
To set the location of the coordinate system	`axes=`
	`NORMAL` in the drawing
	`FRAME` at the lower left edge of the drawing
	`BOXED` at the lower left edge of the drawing with frame
	`NONE` no axes (default)
To alter the calibration of the axes	`tickmarks = [`*m, n, o*`]`
To alter the scaling of the axes	`scaling =`
	`CONSTRAINED` same scale on all axes
	`UNCONSTRAINED` different scale on the axes (default)
To set the number of points to be plotted	`numpoints = `*n* (default is $25^2 = 625$)
To set the observer's viewpoint	`orientation = [`θ, ϕ`]`
	θ, ϕ are given in degrees
	Default values are: $\theta = 45°$, $\phi = 45°$
	Other options are: `FISHEYE`, `NORMAL`, `ORTHOGONAL`

| To set the colour scale | `shading =`
The following models are available:
`XYZ, XY, Z, ZGRAYSCALE,`
`ZHUE, NONE`
Unfortunately the same selection made on different systems produces different results |
| To display graphics | `display3d`(*graphic*) (For this `plots` must be loaded) |

The values of the options must be written either entirely in lower case letters or entirely in upper case.

term	:function term with two variables
var1,var2	:variable descriptor
var1min,var2min	:smallest value for the variable
var1max,var2max	:largest value for the variable
t,u	:parameter
tmin, umin	:smallest value for the parameter
tmax, umax	:largest value for the parameter
$x_1, y_1 \ldots$	:decimal numbers
n, m, o	:whole number greater than 1
graphic	:set, consisting of graphics elements

3D-graphics

6.3   Problems

1. Plot the diagram of function *f* with

$$f(x) = \frac{\sin x}{x}$$

between 0.001 and 2π with labelling.
2. Plot a semicircle with radius 2.
3. Plot a hemisphere with radius 2.

7 Analysis

Computer algebra systems such as *Maple* are a useful and valuable aid for many tasks in analysis; they also save time and even make some tasks in analysis worth attempting. We cannot describe the whole spectrum of applications here, but in the following sections we shall examine a selection of the commands offered by *Maple* for the solution of problems in analysis.

7.1 Derivations

Maple provides the `diff` command for differentiating functions. It enables the derivative of functions of one variable and the partial derivative of a function of several variables to be computed. As the `diff` command can be used for several purposes, it has to be given both the function terms and, separated by a comma, the variable with respect to which it is to be differentiated. We give first some simple examples:

```
> diff(x^n,x);
```

$$\frac{x^n n}{x}$$

```
> simplify(diff(x^n,x));
```

$$x^{n-1} n$$

```
> diff(a*x^n,a);
```

$$x^n$$

In the first example x^n is derived for x; in the second ax^n for a. Next, we give a couple of examples that illustrate *Maple*'s ability to handle functions of one variable:

```
> diff(ln(x^2-u^2),x);
```

$$\frac{2x}{x^2-u^2}$$

```
> diff(7*cos(sqrt(x^3-17*x)),x);
```

$$- \frac{7 \sin(\sqrt{(x^3 - 17x}\,)(3x^2 - 17)}{2\sqrt{x^3 - 17x}}$$

> diff(x^(tan(x^2-v^2)),x);

$$x^{\tan(x^2 - v^2)} \left(2(1 + \tan(x^2 - v^2)^2)x \ln(x) + \frac{\tan(x^2 - v^2)}{x} \right)$$

The example can be pursued further. In many applications, not only the first, but higher derivatives of the function are required. This can be achieved by bracketing the diff command an appropriate number of times. But *Maple* offers simpler ways of writing the command:

> diff(E^(x^2-9),x,x,x);

$$8e^{x^2-9}x^3 + 12e^{x^2-9}x$$

> diff(E^(x^2-9),x$3);

$$8e^{x^2-9}x^3 + 12e^{x^2-9}x$$

With the first form of input diff must be called:

> diff((cos(h(x)))^5,x);

$$-5\cos(h(x))^4 \sin(h(x)) \frac{d}{dx} h(x)$$

This output shows that *Maple* is also master of the rules for differentiating indeterminate symbols (functions). First the determination of

$$\frac{\partial(x^2 - y^2)}{\partial x \partial y}:$$

> diff(x^2-y^2,x);

$$2x$$

Here we only differentiate with respect to x. Now

$$\frac{\partial(x^2-y^2)}{\partial x\partial y}:$$

```
> diff(x^2-y^2,x,y);
```

$$0$$

Because the derivative with respect to *x* contains no *y*, *Maple* gives the correct result, 0.

The next example considers the differentiations with respect to *x* and *x,y* for the function *f* with

$$f(x,y) = e^x \cos y + \sqrt{x^2 - y^2}$$

```
> diff(E^x*cos(y)+sqrt(x^2-y^2),x);
```

$$e^x \cos(y) + \frac{x}{\sqrt{x^2-y^2}}$$

```
> diff(E^x*cos(y)+sqrt(x^2-y^2),x,y);
```

$$-e^x \sin(y) + \frac{xy}{(x^2-y^2)^{3/2}}$$

For many applications a structure is needed that associates with a function its derivative, i.e. an operator or more precisely a differential operator. In *Maple* this is D. To illustrate how it works, we shall first define a function *f*:

```
> f:=x->x^5;
```

$$f := x \rightarrow x^5$$

The application of D to *f*:

```
> D(f);
```

$$x \rightarrow 5x^4$$

Here the first differentiation is output in the form of an assignment. The next example shows what happens when D is applied directly to the last function term:

```
> D(x^5);
```

$$5D(x)x^4$$

Because *Maple* does not know the variables with respect to which it should differentiate, the differentiation is carried out according to the chain rule and output.

The next example illustrates how D operates on predefined functions:

```
> D(cot);
```

$$-1 - \cot^2$$

The output again appears as operator. Any attempt to differentiate a general function term with D fails:

```
> D(cot(x));
Error, (in D) univariate operand expected
```

From the error messsage we can see that D cannot manipulate terms (operators) of this kind. A correct input for this problem would be D(cos)(x). A more detailed explanation of this state of affairs may be found in [1], p. 51.

D can also be applied to functions with several variables. Because in this case only partial differentiations are formed, the number(s) of the D variables must be given as first parameter enclosed between square brackets. As an illustration a function is defined:

```
> f:=(x,y)->sin(x*y);
```

$$f := (x,y) \rightarrow \sin(xy)$$

Now the differentiation function with respect to the first variable (x):

```
> D[1](f);
```

$$(x,y) \rightarrow \cos(xy)y$$

Now the differentiation function with respect to the first variable (x) and the second variable (y):

```
> D[1,2](f);
```

$$(x,y) \rightarrow -\sin(xy)yx + \cos(xy)$$

Differentiation of a function	$\texttt{diff}(f, var)$
Multiple differentiation of a function	$\texttt{diff}(f, var\$ \ number)$ or $\texttt{diff}(f, var, var, ...)$
Partial differentiation of a function	$\texttt{diff}(f, var1, var2, ...)$
Differentiation operator	$\texttt{D}(f)$
Partial differentiation operator	$\texttt{D[n, ...]}(f)$

f	: function
var, var1, var2	: variable(n), for which it is to be differentiated
number	: number of differentiations
n	: whole number greater than zero

Differentiations

7.2   Integrals

In *Maple*, for the analytical determination of integrals the command
$\texttt{integrate}$ or $\texttt{int}$ is used. The first argument given to it is a function term
in one or more variables. The integration variables are then added, separated by
a comma. It is also possible to calculate multiple definite integrals by nesting the
integration command (see the last example in this section).

First we shall look at some examples from the analysis of one variable for
calculating the indefinite integrals, which are also often described as anti-
derivatives (primitives):

```
> int(x^3-x,x);
```

$$\frac{x^4}{4} - \frac{x^2}{2}$$

```
> int(x^2/sqrt(1-x^2),x);
```

$$-\frac{x\sqrt{1-x^2}}{2} + \frac{\arcsin(x)}{2}$$

This example was considered in the previous section.

To determine surfaces that include the curves between 0 and ½ the
integration domain is passed to the $\texttt{int}$ command as second argument:

```
> int(x^2/sqrt(1-x^2),x=0..1/2);
```

$$-\frac{\sqrt{3}}{8}+\frac{\pi}{12}$$

The output shows the exact solution. The decimal approximation is obtained with `evalf` or by inputting an integration limit as a decimal number:

```
> evalf(");
```

$$0.0452930368$$

```
> int(x^s/sqrt(1-x^2),x=0..0.5);
```

$$0.0452930368$$

With *Maple* it is also possible to calculate improper integrals (that is, integrals in which one or both limits take on infinite values):

```
> int(1/E^x,x=0..infinity);
```

$$1$$

In more complex examples limit values are frequently output; these will be examined in the next section.

However, there are also indefinite integrals that cannot be calculated analytically. The next example shows that *Maple* leaves these indefinite integrals unaltered:

```
> int(E^(-x^6),x);
```

$$\int e^{-x^6}dx$$

When we nevertheless require a surface, we describe the required surface in the normal *Maple* syntax and pass the result to the `evalf` command. However, the output is still given as a decimal number:

```
> evalf(int(E^(-x^6),x=0..infinity));
```

$$0.9277193336$$

We can also calculate definite multiple integrals in *Maple* by nesting of the `int` command. The next example shows the procedure for

$$\int\limits_{0}^{\pi/2} \int\limits_{0}^{1} x \, \sin y \, \partial x \partial y :$$

```
> int(int(x*sin(y),x=0..1),y=o..Pi/2);
```

$$\frac{1}{2}$$

```
> int(int(x*sin(y),y=0..Pi/2),x=0..1);
```

$$\frac{1}{2}$$

In the second calculation we see that changing the order of integration does not affect the result.

Indefinite integral of a function	integrate (*f,var*) or int(*f,var*)
Definite integral of a function	integrate (*f,var=varmin..varmax*) or int(*f,var=varmin..varmax*)
Numerical integral of a function	evalf(int(...))
f :function *var* :variable of integration *varmin* :lower limit *varmax* :upper limit	

Integral calculus

7.3   Limits, series and products

In many cases the calculation of boundary values demands greater effort than the theory would lead one to expect. Here *Maple* in many cases offers help in the form of the limit command. The term given as the first argument is the one whose limit is to be considered; the second argument is the variable that tends towards a value:

```
> limit(x^3,x=2);
```

Now some more complicated examples:

```
> limit(x^4*cos(1/x^2),x=0);
```

$$0$$

```
> limit(ln(x^5)/sqrt(x-3),x=infinity);
```

$$0$$

```
> limit(abs(x)/x,x=0);
```

$$\textit{undefined}$$

```
> limit(abs(x)/x,x=0,left);
```

$$-1$$

```
> limit(abs(x)/x,x=0,right);
```

$$1$$

The calculation of these limits with *Maple* is very easy and takes place incredibly quickly.

In addition, the sum command is introduced for the calculation of finite sums. The term to be summed is given as first argument; the second argument is the domain of the summation variable, with its initial and final value.

$$\sum_{0}^{10} \frac{1}{2^i} :$$

```
> sum(1/2^i,i=0..10);
```

$$\frac{2047}{1024}$$

$$\sum_{0}^{n} \frac{1}{2^i} :$$

```
> sum(1/2^i,i=0..n);
```

$$-2\,(1/2)^{n+1} + 2$$

```
> sum(1/2^i,i=0..infinity);
```

$$\sum_{0}^{\infty} \frac{1}{2^i} :$$

2

The examples show that *Maple* calculates sums with number values and variables as well as limits of sums.

Just as one can calculate sums, one can also calculate products. The syntax of the product command is similar to that for sum.

$$\prod_{1}^{5} (1 + \frac{1}{i^2}) :$$

```
> product))1+1/i^2),i=1..5);
```

$$\frac{221}{72}$$

$$\prod_{1}^{n}(1 + \frac{1}{i^2}) :$$

```
> product((1+1/i^2),i=1..n);
```

$$\frac{\Gamma(n+1-I)\Gamma(n+1+I)}{\Gamma(n+1)^2\Gamma(1-I)\Gamma(1+I)}$$

The result is here described in terms of the gamma function ($\Gamma(n)$). For natural numbers the value is: $\Gamma(n+1) = n! = 1.2...n$. Now to determine the limit value

$$\prod_{1}^{\infty}(1 + \frac{1}{i^2}) :$$

```
> product((1+1/i^2),i=1..infinity);
```

$$\prod_{i=1}^{\infty} 1 + i^{-2}$$

Because this only returns the input, the next attempt is to pass the finite product to the limit value command limit, leaving the upper limit at infinity:

```
> limit(product((1+1/i^2),i=1..n),n=infinity);
```

$$\frac{1}{\Gamma(1-I)\Gamma(1+I)}$$

Lastly, in this section we introduce the `series` command for calculating power series. As first argument the command expects the term to be developed, as second the location around which expansion is to be made, and as third, optionally, the smallest power of the remainder (the default is 6). As an example we introduce the cosine series from the null to the fourth power:

```
> series(cos(x),x=0);
```

$$1 - \frac{1}{2}x^2 + \frac{1}{24}x^4 + O(x^6)$$

Now the same series, in which the smallest power of the remainder is 10:

```
> series(cos(x),x=0,10);
```

$$1 - \frac{1}{2}x^2 + \frac{1}{24}x^4 - \frac{1}{720}x^6 + \frac{1}{40320}x^8 + O(x^{10})$$

In many cases, with these power series one can calculate as with functions, that is, differentiate, integrate, etc.:

```
> diff(",x);
```

$$-x + \frac{1}{6}x^3 - \frac{1}{120}x^5 + \frac{1}{5040}x^7 + O(x^9)$$

```
> int(",x);
```

$$-\frac{1}{2}x^2 + \frac{1}{24}x^4 - \frac{1}{720}x^6 + \frac{1}{40320}x^8 + O(x^{10})$$

For continued calculations (multiplication, division, etc.) with power series *Maple* offers the supplementary package `powerseries`.

Boundary value of a term	`limit` (*term, var = var0*)
Sum	`sum(`*term,var=varmin,.. varmax*`)`
Product	`product(`*term,var=varmin.. varmax*`)`
Power series	`series(`*f,var=var0, varh*`)`

f	:function
term	:function term
var	:variable
varmin	:lower bound
varmax	:upper bound
var0	:fixed location for the variable
varh	:highest power of the variable

Boundary value, sums and products

7.4 Differential equations

Much has been, and will be, written about the solution of differential equations (DEs). Even the possibilities offered by *Maple* are sufficient for one or more books, because *Maple* contains one command for the analytical solution and one for the numerical solution of DEs. In this section we shall show some examples of how simple linear DEs can be solved with *Maple*.

The command used is `dsolve`; its syntax is similar to that of `solve`. To solve the equation $f'(x) = kf(x)$:

```
> dsolve(diff(f(x),x)=k*f(x),f(x));
```

$$f(x) = e^{kx} \_C1$$

Here the expected solution $f(x) = c_1 e^{kx}$ is obtained, where the constant c_1 needs to be determined because of other conditions (for example, initial value). If we want to solve the DE for a fixed initial value (say 5), this initial condition can be given to the `dsolve` command as a further equation:

```
> solve({diff(f(x),x)=k*f(x),f(0)=5},f(x));
```

$$f(x) = 5e^{kx}$$

As this input shows, the `dsolve` command expects at least two arguments: the first being a set with equations, then a set with the functions for which the equation is to be solved, and thirdly options can be added. The available options are as follows:

`explicit` : forces, where possible, the closed representation of the solution
`laplace` : uses Laplace transforms in the solution
`series` : uses power series in the solution
`numeric` : solves the DE numerically

The set that contains the equations can contain both differential and ordinary equations. The latter are generally used to describe the initial conditions.

Next, the DE is considered for damped oscillation:

```
> dsolve(m*diff(f(x),x$2)+r*diff(f(x),x)+k*f(x)=0,f(x));
```

$$f(x) = \_C1\,e^{-\frac{(r-\sqrt{r^2-4km})\,x}{2m}} + \_C2\,e^{-\frac{(r+\sqrt{r^2-4km})\,x}{2m}}$$

The solution is calculated correctly as the sum of two *e*-functions, where the exponents of the *e*-functions may be complex. The following example investigates the DE of the forced oscillation:

```
>
dsolve(m*diff(f(x),x$2)+r*diff(f(x),x)+k*f(x)=a*sin(b
*x),f(x));
```

$$
\begin{aligned}
f(x) = (\,&\_C1\ \%2b^4m^2 - ma\sin(bx)b^2 - ab\cos(bx)r \\
&+ \_C2\ \%3b^4m^2 + \_C1\ \%2r^2b^2 + \_C2\ \%3r^2b^2 + \_C1\ \%2k^2 \\
&+ \_C2\ \%3k^2 - 2\_C2\ \%3b^2mk + a\sin(bx)k - 2\_C1\ \%2b^2mk) \\
&(r^2b^2 + k^2 - 2kmb^2 + b^4m^2)^{-1}
\end{aligned}
$$

$$\%1 := \sqrt{r^2 - 4km}$$

$$\%2 := e^{\,[-(r-\%1)x/2m]}$$

$$\%3 := e^{\,[-(r+\%1)x/2m]}$$

Here again the expected solutions are correctly presented. To make the display more readable, as with equations some parts are provided with the % sign and separated out.

For the numerical solution of differential equations, *Maple* offers the numeric option for the dsolve command. However, because the application of this command requires even more experience of differential equations and the interpretation of their solutions, we refer interested readers to the *Maple* handbook ([3], p. 183).

To solve differential equations	$\mathtt{dsolve(\{}ls = rs...\mathtt{\}}, f\mathtt{(}var\mathtt{)}, \textit{options}\mathtt{)}$

ls :left side of equation
rs :right side of equation
f :function sought or list of sought functions
var :independent solution variable

Solution of differential equations

7.5   Problems

1. Find the derivative:

$$\frac{d(e^{4-x^2}\cos x)}{dx}$$

2. Find the partial derivative with respect to x and y:

$$\frac{\partial(e^{4-x^2}\sin y)}{\partial x\partial y}$$

3. Find the indefinite integral:

$$\int\sqrt{x^2 - 2x + 5}dx$$

4. Find the definite integral:

$$\int_0^5 \sqrt{x^2 - 2x + 5}dx$$

Also, obtain a decimal approximation for the integral.

5. Solve the differential equation

$$f'(x) - x^2(f(x))^2 = x^2$$

8 Simple programs

In this chapter we shall not present a comprehensive guide to building giant program packages, but try to show by means of some small examples how to make everyday working with *Maple* a little easier. Because programming in *Maple* closely resembles programming in a high-level procedural language such as C, Pascal, etc., we shall introduce the following basic concepts:

- linear programs
- programs with branches
- programs with repeat structures

In particular, for programmers with knowledge of a high-level language it should be mentioned that *Maple* uses three-value logic, in contrast to the more general two-value logic. In the conventional two-value logic of programming languages there are only two possibilites – the values `true` or `false` – for the truth value of an expression. *Maple*, however, recognises a third value which states that no decision is possible – `FAIL`. This must be borne in mind when programming, especially when the truth value of an expression is important for further program runs.

In this chapter some fundamental programming techniques in *Maple* are explained by means of an example. The example chosen is the proof of an equation.

8.1   Linear programs

In section 4.2 it was shown how to carry out the verification of solutions of an equation. For this the individual solutions had to be input into the equation with some keying cost. In order to reduce this, the individual commands are assembled into a new command, called `TEST`. The grouping of individual commands is described as a procedure, and the appropriate *Maple* command is `proc`. In order to try out the command immediately, we shall define an equation:

```
> EQ:=sqrt(5*x-1)=x-5;
```

$$\sqrt{5x-1} = x-5$$

Now the procedure:

```
> TEST:=proc(XL)               # XL : a solution of the
                                    equation
> local LS,RS;                 # declare local variables
> LS:=subs(x=XL,lhs(EQ));      # evaluate left side
> RS:=subs(x=XL,rhs(EQ));      # evaluate right side
> end;                         # end procedure

TEST := proc(XL)
           local LS,RS;
                LS := subs(x = XL,lhs(EQ));
                RS := subs(x = XL,rhs(EQ))
           end
```

As can be seen, the procedure is input like a normal sequence of commands, that is, each command must conclude with a semicolon. The comments included after the # sign are to assist readability; they do not have to be input. After the input *Maple* outputs the formatted sequence of commands. To avoid problems of multi-assignment of a variable during a *Maple* session, all variables that are only required in the procedure should be declared as local variables. The assignment for local variables is only valid within the procedure; they are invalid outside the procedure.

When inputting procedures, the following should be observed:

---

1. Assign a procedure name
2. Define a variable to call the procedure (solution XL above)
3. Conclude commands correctly with a semicolon or colon (no semicolon may precede command words such as end, fi, od, else, etc.)
4. End the procedure with end;

Inputting procedures

Now the test:

```
> TEST(2);
```

$$-3$$

We see that only the value of the right side is output; the other is missing. This is not a programming error, but a property of *Maple* procedures, which only return the last command. One possibility of getting round this is the direct output of the required value with the command print. An application shows the extension of the TEST procedure:

```
> TEST:=proc(XL)
> local LS,RS;
> LS:=subs(x=XL,lhs(EQ));
> RS:=subs(x=XL,rhs(EQ));
> print(LS,RS);
> end;
TEST := proc(XL)
            local LS,RS;
                LS := subs(x = XL,lhs(EQ));
                RS := subs(x = XL,rhs(EQ));
                print(LS,RS)
            end
```

The test for the equation (EQ) for the value 2:

```
> TEST(2);
```

$$\sqrt{9},-3$$

Now both values are output. To make the output more readable, in the following example additional comments are included. These are given, enclosed within opening quotes ('), to the print command:

```
> TEST:=proc(XL)
> local LS,RS;
> LS:=subs(x=XL,lhs(EQ));
> RS:=subs(x=XL,rhs(EQ));
> print('left side :',LS,'right side :',RS);
> end;
TEST := proc(XL)
            local LS,RS;
                LS := subs(x = XL,lhs(EQ));
                RS := subs(x = XL,rhs(EQ));
                print('left side :',LS,'right side :',RS)
            end
```

```
> TEST(2);
```

left side $:,\sqrt{9}$*, right side* $:, -3$

```
> TEST(13);
```

left side $:,\sqrt{64}$*, right side*$:, 4$

This output is indeed easier to read, but users of this command must compare the values for themselves to establish whether a value is a solution or not. The next section shows a realisation of this problem.

8.2   Branching programs

For decisions, *Maple* offers the if ... then command. Its complete syntax is as follows:

```
if      condition    then                 sequence of commands
|       elif         condition            sequence of commands |
|       elif         condition            sequence of commands |
|       ...                                                    |
|       else          sequence of commands |
fi;
```

```
condition              :    expression, whose truth value can be tested
sequence of commands   :    sequence of Maple commands (the correct
                            syntax must be observed)
```

The optional parts of the sequence of commands in the above are enclosed within vertical lines (|) .

It should also be noted that because of the three-value logic the following sequences of commands must not provide any identical solutions:

```
if          condition    then   sequence of commands1
                         else   sequence of commands2
fi;
if not      condition    then   sequence of commands2
                         else   sequence of commands1
fi;
```

if ... then

Because in most cases the sequence of commands if .. then .. fi; or if .. then .. else .. fi; are sufficient, these will be examined more closely. As can be seen, all decisions must terminate with the fi command. In all cases, after if the expression is tested to establish whether it is true. If it is, then the commands after then are carried out. If another else is present, then the sequence of commands after it is carried out, that is, when the if condition is not true. What significance does this have for the application of the test in the previous section?

The condition that has to be tested here is whether the left side (LS) and the right side (RS) agree at the start of a solution, or briefly LS=RS. This produces the following decision schematic:

If LS = RS	Output: XL is a solution
otherwise	Output: XL is not a solution

To test this, there is first no binding into a procedure. Because the equation was already defined in the previous section, only the variables LS, RS and XL need to be defined:

```
> LS:=subs(x=XL,lhs(EQ)):
> RS:=subs(x=XL.rhs(EQ)):
> XL:=2;
```

Now follows the input of the question:

```
> if LS=RS    then print(XL,' is a solution ');
>             else print(XL,' is not a solution ');
> fi;
```

2, *is not a solution*

Now the investigation for the second solution (13):

```
> XL:=13;
> if LS=RS    then print(XL,' is a solution ');
>             else print(XL,' is not a solution ');
> fi;
```

13, *is not a solution*

If we look at the examples in section 4.2, we can see that 13 is a solution. Moreover, we see there that the comparison $\sqrt{64} = 8$ must be carried out. However, for *Maple* these are different objects. On the left side there is a root (a symbol) and on the right side a number. In order for *Maple* to recognise both sides as equal values, both sides must be simplified with the simplify command:

```
> XL:='XL';   # Variable XL is freed — see chapter 2
```

```
> LS:=simplify(subs(x=XL,lhs(EQ)));
> RS:=simplify(subs(x=XL,rhs(EQ)));
> XL:=13;
> if LS + RS then print(XL,' is a solution ');
>            else print(XL,' is not a solution ');
> fi;
```

13, *is a solution*

The next input tests whether a correct checking is obtained for 2 also:

```
> XL:=2;
> if LS = RS then print(XL,' is a solution ');
>            else print(XL,' is not a solution ');
> fi;
```

2, *is not a solution*

Since everything behaves as expected, this sequence of commands can be defined as in the previous section:

```
> TEST:=proc(XL)
> local LS,RS;
> LS:=simplify(subs(x=XL,lhs(EQ)));
> RS:=simplify(subs(x=XL,rhs(EQ)));
> if LS = RS then print(XL,' is a solution ');
>              else print(XL,' is not a solution ');
> fi;
> end;
TEST := proc(XL)
       local LS,RS;
           LS:=simplify(subs(x=XL,lhs(EQ)));
           RS:=simplify(subs(x=XL,rhs(EQ)));
           if LS = RS then print(XL,' is a solution ')
                      else print(XL,' is not a solution ')
           fi
       end
```

The approach presented here of first testing parts on the normal input plane before including them in a procedure has advantages for independent programming work, because one is generally dealing with smaller and therefore more comprehensible sections of program and the output is obtained immediately after each input.

If an equation now has several solutions, the TEST command must be called for every solution. The call with a list of solutions would certainly be a simplification. The next section shows the conversion of this kind of problem.

8.3   Programs with loops

For a programmer, a loop is the repetition of a program or of part of a program. This construct is well suited to the kind of problem that was described at the end of the previous section. Before it is demonstrated we should first review the complete syntax of the *Maple* commands for repeat structures:

| for *var* || from *expr* | | by *expr* || to *expr* || while *expr* |
        do
                Sequence of commands
        od;

or

| for *var* || in || while *expr* |
        do
                Sequence of commands
        od;

expr	:	expression
var	:	variable descriptor
Sequence of commands	:	series of *Maple* commands (correct *Maple* syntax must be observed)

The optional parts of the commands sequence are indicated in the above summary enclosed between vertical lines (|). Thus a very free approach to programming is possible, albeit running the risk of errors if precise attention to structure is not maintained. For this reason the following special cases are of interest:

Number loops
        for *var* from *expr* by *expr* to *expr*
            do
                    Sequence of commands
            od;

Repetition of an assignment
        while *expr*
            do
                    Sequence of commands
            od;

Working through a list
        for *var* in *expr*
            do
                    Sequence of commands
            od;

for...

First we shall show how all tests can be carried out with a number loop. For this all solutions are grouped into a list:

```
> LIST:=[2,13]:
```

With the aid of LIST the problem solution can be formulated in the following way:

Execute for *i* from 1 through length of LIST as follows:	
	make the test (sequence of commands, see above)

at each pass, counter *i* should be incremented by 1.
Or:

for *i* from 1 by 1 to nops(LIST)	
	do
	make the test
	od;

The appropriate *Maple* syntax is:

```
> for i from 1 to nops(LIST) do
> XL:=op(i,LIST);
> LS:=simplify(subs(x=XL,lhs(EQ)));
> RS:=simplify(subs(x=XL,rhs(EQ)));
> if LS = RS    then print(XL,'is a solution ')
>               else print(XL,'is not a solution ')
> fi;
> od;
```

$$XL := 2$$
$$LS := 3$$
$$RS := -3$$
2, *is not a solution*
$$XL := 13$$
$$LS := 8$$
$$RS := 8$$
13, *is a solution*

The assignment by 1 must not be carried out, because *Maple* automatically increases numerical variables by 1 when no other value is provided. A somewhat simpler description of the solution can be obtained with the for .. in construct:

```
> for XL in LIST do
> LS:=simplify(subs(x=XL,lhs(EQ)));
> RS:=simplify(subs(x=XL,rhs(EQ)));
> if    LS = RS then print(XL,'is a solution ')
>               else print(XL,'is not a solution ')
> fi;
> od;
```

This sequence of commands can then be grouped as a procedure, to which a list with solutions is given:

```
> TEST;=proc(LIST)
> local LS,RS,XL;
> for XL in LIST do
>  LS:=simplify(subs(x=XL,lhs(EQ)));
>  RS:=simplify(subs(x=XL,rhs(EQ)));
>  if   LS = RS then print(XL,'is a solution ')
>              else print(XL,'is not a solution ')
>  fi;
> od;
> end;

TEST :=
  proc(LIST)
  local LS,RS,XL;
      for XL in LIST do
          LS:=simplify(subs(x = XL,lhs(EQ)));
          RS:=simplify(subs(x = XL,rhs(EQ)));
          if   LS = RS then print(XL,'is a solution ')
                      else print(XL,'is not a solution ') fi
      od
  end
```

If we call this procedure with a list:

```
> TEST([2,13]);
```

$$2, \textit{is not a solution}$$
$$13, \textit{is a solution}$$

If no lists are given to this procedure, errors occur:

```
> TEST(2,13);
```

$$2, \textit{is not a solution}$$

Because the parameter given was not a list, only a value is tested. In many cases this depends on the previously used commands in a *Maple* session.

The type command can be used to test for a type. The following types are normally available:

*	**	+	.	..	<
<=	<>	=	PLOT	PLOT3D	RootOf
TEXT	^	algebraic	algext	algfun	algnum
algnumext	and	anything	arctrig	argcheck	arithop
array	boolean	complex	constant	defn	dot
equation	evenfunc	evenodd	expanded	facint	factorial
float	fraction	function	indexed	integer	laurent
linear	list	listlist	mathfunc	matrix	monomial
name	not	nothing	numeric	operator	or
point	polynom	posneg	posnegint	primeint	procedure
radext	radfun	radfunext	radical	radnum	radnumext
range	rational	ratpoly	realcons	relation	scalar
series	set	sqrt	square	string	structure
surface	table	taylor	trig	type	uneval
union	vector				

The `type(LIST,list)` command allows investigation of whether the parameter to be given is a list. If this is not the case, the procedure should be terminated with an error message. This can be programmed with the ERROR command. The error message is passed to it enclosed within single opening quotes (`). The full procedure is:

```
> TEST;=proc(LIST)
> local LS,RS,XL;
> if not type(LIST,list) then
>     ERROR(` Argument must be a list. `) fi;
> for XL in LIST do
> LS:=simplify(subs(x=XL,lhs(EQ)));
> RS:=simplify(subs(x=XL,rhs(EQ)));
> if   LS = RS   then print(XL,`is a solution `)
>                 else print(XL,`is not a solution `)
> fi;
> od;
> end;
  TEST :=
    proc(LIST)
    local LS,RS,XL;
      if not type(LIST,list) then
         ERROR(` Argument must be a list. `) fi;
      for XL in LIST do
         LS:=simplify(subs(x = XL,lhs(EQ)));
         RS:=simplify(subs(x = XL,rhs(EQ)));
         if   LS = RS   then print(XL,`is a solution `)
                        else print(XL,`is not a solution
`)
         fi
      od
    end
```

Calling with a list yields the same results.
   Now one with errors:

```
> TEST(2);
Error, (in TEST)  Argument must be a list.
```

Up to now, first the equation had to be solved and then the test was carried out. Clearly, it is simpler to use a command that carries out both. It would have to:

- Solve the equation
- Group the solutions in a list
- Carry out the test

It is only necessary to give an equation to this command:

```
> PSOLVE:=proc(EQ)
> local LS,RS,LIST,XL;
> if not type(EQ,equation) then
>       ERROR(' Argument must be an equation. ') fi;
> LIST:=[solve(EQ,x)];
> for XL in LIST do
>  LS:=simplify(subs(x=XL,lhs(EQ)));
>  RS:=simplify(subs(x=XL,rhs(EQ)));
>  if   LS = RS then print(XL,'is a solution ')
>                 else print(XL,'is not a solution ')
>  fi;
> od;
> end;

PSOLVE :=
   proc(EQ)
   local LS,RS,LIST,XL;
      if not type(EQ,equation) then
         ERROR(' Argument must be an equation. ') fi;
      LIST := [solve(EQ,x)];
      for XL in LIST do
         LS:=simplify(subs(x = XL,lhs(EQ)));
         RS:=simplify(subs(x = XL,rhs(EQ)));
         if   LS = RS then print(XL,'is a solution ')
                        else print(XL,'is not a solution ') fi
      od
   end
```

These tests then follow:

```
> PSOLVE(sqrt(5*x-1)=x-5);
```

> 2, *is not a solution*
> 13, *is a solution*

```
> PSOLVE(x^2-5*x=6);
```

> 6, *is a solution*
> −1, *is a solution*

When the result consists of several solutions the output can be somewhat confusing. In such cases it is sensible to arrange for all solutions to be written as a list that is output at the end of the procedure:

```
> if not type(EQ,equation) then
>     ERROR(` Argument must be a equation. `) fi;
> LIST:=[solve(EQ,x)];
> LLIST:=[ ];
> for XL in LIST do
>  LS:=simplify(subs(x=XL,lhs(EQ)));
>  RS:=simplify(subs(x=XL,rhs(EQ)));
>  if LS = RS then LLIST:=[op(LLIST),XL]
>  fi;
> od;
> print('The solutions are : ');
> print(LLIST);
> end;
PSOLVE := proc(EQ)
    local LS,RS,LIST,LLIST,XL;
        if not type(EQ,equation) then
            ERROR(` Argument must be an equation. `) fi;
        LIST := [solve(EQ,x)];
        LLIST := [];
        for XL in LIST do
            LS:=simplify(subs(x = XL,lhs(EQ)));
            RS:=simplify(subs(x = XL,rhs(EQ)));
            if LS = RS then LLIST := [op(LLIST),XL] fi
        od;
        print('The solutions are : ');
        print(LLIST)
    end
```

This procedure can be further enlarged. For example, one possibility might be to allow free choice of solution variables. More information about programming in *Maple* may be found in [3], p. 115 and [4].

The command for saving one's own commands is save:

```
> save PSOLVE , 'mydat.m ';
```

On inputting the above, it must not be forgotten to include the comma after the variable, with the data name enclosed within single opening quotes.

For loading there is the read command:

```
> read mydat.m;
PSOLVE := proc(EQ)
        local LS,RS,LIST,LLIST,XL;
            if not type(EQ,equation) then
                ERROR(` Argument must be an equation. `) fi;
            LIST := [solve(EQ,x)];
            LLIST := [];
            for XL in LIST do
                LS:=simplify(subs(x = XL,lhs(EQ)));
                RS:=simplify(subs(x = XL,rhs(EQ)));
                if LS = RS then LLIST := [op(LLIST),XL] fi
            od;
            print('The solutions are : ');
            print(LLIST)
        end
```

8.4 Problems

1. Write a program that determines the following for a function:

   - The roots of $(f(x) = 0)$
   - The critical points $(f'(x) = 0)$
   - The turning points $(f''(x) = 0)$

   In addition, the graph of the function should be drawn.

2. Test the following program, which determines the stem function of rational integral functions. Find out which rules were programmed. (The idea for this program comes from [4], on p. 25.)

```
> INT:=proc(TERM,x)
> local u,v;
> if not type(TERM,algebraic) then ERROR(' 1.
> Argument must be a rational integral term ') fi;
> if not type(x, name) the ERROR(' 2. Argument must
         be a variable ') fi;
> if type(TERM,numeric) then TERM*x;
> elif type(TERM,name) then if TERM = x then x^2/2
>                                     else TERM*x fi;
> elif type(TERM,'+') then map(INT,TERM,x);
> elif type(TERM.'*') then u:=op(1,TERM);
                            v:=op(2,TERM);
> u*INT(v,x);
> elif type(TERM,anything^integer) then u:=op(1,TERM);
>                                       v:=op(2,TERM);
> if u='x' then  u^(v+1)/(v+1)   ; else TERM*x fi;
> fi:
> end;
```

Appendix A   Installation on PCs

Maple is normally delivered on several numbered diskettes. This appendix describes how to install an executable *Maple* program suite using these diskettes. *Maple* is available for text or windows based user interfaces on many computers, ranging from PCs to mainframes (see Preface); we shall therefore describe the installation for PCs, since for other types of system the user does not normally have to install software. Before embarking on the installation, security copies of the original diskettes should be made. The following description applies to MS-DOS machines.

Unpack your diskettes and, using the MS-DOS `diskcopy` command, make copies of all the diskettes provided according to the normal format of your machine — 3.5 in or 5.25 in. Place the first overwrite protected original diskette in the correct drive, usually `a:` or `b:`. The copy command required for each diskette is:

For Drive `a:` `diskcopy a: a:`
For Drive `b:` `diskcopy b: b:`

If your PC has two similar drives, the command can be altered to:

For two drives: `diskcopy a: b:`

For this the original diskette must be in drive `a:` and the new security diskette in drive `b:`.

Once copies of all the diskettes have been made, the originals should be stored in a safe place.

The accompanying booklet *Getting Started* contains on the first page a precise description of all commands that are required for the range of computers (PC, Macintosh, Amiga, UNIX systems, etc.). Of special interest in the booklet is the section entitled 'Installation Procedure'. For smaller machines such as the PC and the Macintosh it is sufficient to insert the first diskette supplied into the corresponding drive and start the `Install` program. With other systems further procedures are required; these are fully described in the section 'Installation Procedure' as a step-by-step sequence. After calling `Install` the program runs automatically, or a selection menu appears. On MS-DOS machines this appears as follows:

Maple V Release 2 for DOS and Windows — Installation Facility

```
Install from Diskette Drive:        B      (10100K)
Install to Drive and Directory:     C:\MAPLEV2

Install DOS Version?                Y      (950K)
Modify AUTOEXEC.BAT File?            Y
Disk with AUTOEXEC.BAT File:        C

Install Windows Version?            Y      (1450K)
Windows 3.1 Drive and Directory:    C:\WINDOWS

Install Share Library?              Y      (3600K)
Install Tutorial?                   Y      (150K)

Remove Release 1?                   N      (-8050K)
Maple V R1 Drive and Directory:     C:\MAPLEV

↑,↓ — Select Field      ←,→ — Move Cursor      F3 — Begin
Installation            ESc — Cancel
```

Here the user is offered some options; help can be obtained from the information in the last line. Thus the installation can be initiated by striking function key F3. The program then prompts the user to insert the appropriate installation diskettes. At the end of the installation the serial number must be provided. This data must be taken and input from the first installation diskette. If one neglects to do this, *Maple* is liable to behave unpredictably, for example by persistently requesting input of the serial number.

After installation is completed, a further report is usually displayed. Under MS-DOS this appears as follows:

```
Maple V Release 2 for DOS and Windows — Installation Facility
Install from Diskette Drive:        B  (10100K)
Ins
The installation was completed. Please reboot your computer
now. (Ins950K)
Modify AUTOEXEC.BAT File?            Y
Disk with AUTOEXEC.BAT File:        C

Install Windows Version?            Y  (1450K)
Windows 3.1 Drive and Directory*    C:\WINDOWS

Install Share Library?              Y  (3600K)
Install Tutorial?                   Y  (150K)

Remove Release 1?                   N  (-8050K)
```

```
*You may want to edit it to remove any redundant PATH
   statements.
Adding C:\MAPLEV2\BIN directory to PATH
Adding SET MAPLELIB statement to AUTOEXEC.BAT
Scanning CONFIG.SYS for possible problems.
Creating MAPLEV2.INI file in Windows directory
Inserting serial number in DOS version.
Inserting serial number in Windows version.

↑,↓ — Select Field      ←,→ — Move Cursor      F3 — Begin
Installation            ESc — Cancel
```

Once the machine is rebooted, *Maple* can be started as described in section 1.1.

Appendix B List of commands

abs(*z*)
> calculates the modulus of a complex number or the absolute value of a real number.

addcols(*matrix,s1,s2,factor*)
> adds two columns (*s1, s2*) of a matrix (*matrix*). As an option, the first column can be multiplied by a factor (*factor*). (Command from the **linalg** package.)

addrows(*matrix,z1,z2,factor*)
> adds two rows (*z1, z2*) of a matrix (*matrix*). As an option, the first row can be multiplied by a factor (*factor*). (Command from the **linalg** package.)

arccos(*x*)
> calculates the inverse cosine (arccos *x*).

arccot(*x*)
> calculates the inverse cotangent (arccot *x*).

arccsc(*x*)
> calculates the inverse cosecant (arccsc *x*).

arcsec(*x*)
> calculates the inverse secant (arcsec *x*).

arcsin(*x*)
> calculates the inverse sine (arcsin *x*).

arctan(*x*)
> calculates the inverse tangent (arctan *x*).

array(*option, index domain(s), list*)
> describes an array. The options discussed in the book are:
> **antisymmetric** for antisymmetric
> **diagonal** for arrays only occupied in the diagonals
> **identity** for the identity matrix
> **sparse** for sparse arrays

augment(*matrix1, matrix2*)
> combines two matrices into a single column. (Command from the **linalg** package.)

coeff(*expr, var*)
  determines the coefficient of the variable *var* in the expression *expr*.

col(*matrix, n*)
  provides the *n*th column of a matrix (*matrix*). (Command from the **linalg** package.)

combine(*expr, option*)
  groups together the single terms of an expression.

concat(*matrix1, matrix2*)
  combines two matrices columnwise into one. (Command from the **linalg** package.)

conjugate(*z*)
  calculates the complex conjugate of a complex number.

convert(*expr, form, option(s)*)
  converts structures between one another. In this book the following are discussed:

  convert(*z*,**polar**) conversion from cartesian to polar coordinates.
  convert(*angle***degrees**,*radians*) conversion from degrees into radians.
  convert(*expr*,**parfrac**,*x*) separates a rational expression into partial fractions.
  convert(*list*,**array**) converts a list into an array.
  convert(*list*,**vector**) converts a list into a vector.

copyinto(*matrix1, matrix2,m,n*)
  copies the input parts (*m,n*) of the first matrix into the second. (Command from the **linalg** package.)

cos(*x*)
  calculates the cosine (cos *x*).

cot(*x*)
  calculates the cotangent (cot *x*).

crossprod(*v1,v2*)
  calculates the cross product of two vectors. (Command from the **linalg** package.)

csc(*x*)
  calculates the cosecant (csc *x*).

D(*f*)
  Derivative operator.

D[*n*](*f*)
  Partial derivative operator.

degree(*expr,var*)
  determines the degree of a polynomial with respect to the variable *var*.

delcols(*matrix, s*)
  deletes a column from a matrix (*matrix*). (Command from the **linalg** package.)

delrows(*matrix, z*)
  deletes a row from a matrix (*matrix*). (Command from the **linalg** package.)

denom(*expr*)
  provides the denominator of a fraction.

det(*m*)
  calculates the determinant of a square matrix. (Command from the **linalg** package.)

diff(*f,var,...*)
  differentiates the function term with respect to the given variable. Can also be used for partial differentiation.

Digits:=*number*
  fixes the number of decimal places for numerical calculations.

display(*graphic*)
  displays the graphic on the specified output channel. (Command from the **plots** package.)

display3d(*graphic*)
  displays the graphic on the specified output channel. (Command from the **plots** package.)

dotprod(*v1,v2*)
  calculates the scalar product of two vectors. (Command from the **linalg** package.)

dsolve({*ls = rs...*}, *f*(*var*), *options*)
  solves an ordinary differential equation. The following options are available:

  explicit forces, where possible, the closed representation of the solution
  laplace uses Laplace transforms to solve
  numeric solves the differential equation numerically
  series uses power series to solve

eigenvals(*matrix*)
  calculates the eigenvalues of a square matrix. (Command from the **linalg**

package.)

entries(*name*)
outputs the values of previously assigned entries of an array or a table.

evalb(*expr*)
evaluates Boolean terms.

evalc(*expr*)
calculates complex terms.

evalf(*expr, places*)
calculates a decimal approximation of terms.

evalm(*expr*)
calculates expressions that contain arrays (vectors, matrices, etc.).

exp(*x*)
calculates the exponential function (e^x).

expand(*expr*)
expands and summarises a term. In rational expressions only the numerator is expanded.

factor(*expr*)
factorises a term. In rational expressions both numerator and denominator are factorised.

Factor(*expr, K*)
factorises a term for a required body *K*.

| **for** *var* || from *expr* ||by *expr* || to *expr* || **while** *expr* |
do *sequence of commands* **od;**
general description of loops, or:

|**for** *var* ||**in** ||**while** *expr* | **do** *sequence of commands* **od;**
general description of loops. The instructions shown between the vertical bars are optional.

fsolve({*ls = rs...*}, *var, options*)
solves an equation or a set of equations numerically for given solution variables. The **complex** options also allows complex solutions to be determined.

gausselim(*matrix*)
carries out Gaussian elimination for a matrix. (Command from the **linalg** package.)

if *condition* **then** *sequence of commands*
    | **elif** *condition* **then** *sequence of commands* |
    | **elif** *condition* **then** *sequence of commands* |

   ...
    | **else** *sequence of commands* | **fi;**

> general description of a conditional assignment. The data between the
> vertical bars (|) is optional.

ifactor(*n*)
> determines the prime factors of the number *n* with the corresponding
> exponents.

Im(*z*)
> calculates the imaginary part of a complex number.

indices(*name*)
> outputs the indices of already assigned elements of an array or a table.

int
> see **integrate**

integrate(*f, var*)
> indefinite integral of a function.

integrate(*f, var=varmin..varmax*)
> definite integral of a function.

intersection
> intersects sets.

inverse(*matrix*)
> calculates the inverse of a square matrix. (Command from the **linalg**
> package.)

lcoeff(*expr, var*)
> determines the highest coefficient of the variable *var* in the expression *expr*.

lhs(*equation*)
> determines the left side of an equation.

limit(*term, var = var0, direction*)
> calculates the limit of a term. The following approximations are possible
> (*direction*): **left, right, real, complex**.

linsolve(*matrix, vector*)
> solves a linear system of equations with the coefficient matrix (*matrix*) and
> the target vector (*vector*). (Command from the **linalg** package.)

ln(*x*)
> calculates the natural logarithmic function (ln *x*).

log[Basis](*x*)
> calculates the logarithmic function to base *b* ($\log_b x$).

map(*f, expr*)
> applies the function (procedure) *f* to an expression.

member(*element, set*)
> tests whether an element is contained in a set.

minus
> creates the difference set.

mulcol(*matrix, s, expr*)
> multiplies the columns (*s*) of a matrix (*matrix*) by an expression. (Command from the **linalg** package.)

mulrow(*matrix, z, expr*)
> multiplies the row (*z*) of a matrix (*matrix*) by an expression. (Command from the **linalg** package.)

nop(*expr*)
> determines the number of operands of an expression.

normal(*expr*)
> summarises a rational expression.

numer(*expr*)
> provides the numerator of a rational expression.

op(*n, expr*)
> determines the *n*th operand of an expression. A domain for operands can be provided as first argument (op(m..n,...)).

Pi
> *Maple* symbol for π.

plot({ *set* }, *var=varmin..varmax, options*)
> plots the graph of one or more functions.

plot({[*x(t),y(t),t=tmin..tmax*]}, *var=varmin..varmax, options*)
> plots the graph of one or more parametrised curves.

plot({[[x_1,y_1],[x_2,y_2]...], *var=varmin..varmax, options*)
> plots the graph of a table. In this book the following options for **plot** are discussed:

style= sets the plot style
POINT plots points only
LINE joins up points by a curve (default)
PATCH joins points by a straight line
title='text' describes a graph
axes= sets the location of the coordinate system
NORMAL in the graph (default)
FRAME at the lower left border of the graph
BOXED at the lower left border of the graph with frame
NONE no axes
xtickmarks = n alter calibration for the x-axis
ytickmarks = n alter calibration for the y-axis
scaling = alter the scaling of the axes
CONSTRAINED same scale on both axes
UNCONSTRAINED different scale on the axes (default)
numpoints = n set number of points to be plotted (default is 25 to 49)

plot3D(*term, var1=varmin1.. varmax1, var2=varmin2..varmax2, options*)
plots the graph of a function.

plot3D([*x(u,t),y(u,t),z(u,t)*], *t=tmin..tmax, u=umin..umax, options*)
plots the graph of a parametrised surface. In this book the following options
for **plot3D** are discussed:

style = sets the plot style
HIDDEN hidden lines are not plotted (default)
PATCH fills a surface with polygons
PATCHNOGRID the polygons are plotted without a wire frame
Other options are **POINT, WIREFRAME, CONTOUR, PATCHCONTOUR, LINE**
title='text' describes a graph
axes= set location of the coordinate system
NORMAL in the plot
FRAME at the lower left border of the graph
BOXED at the lower left border of the graph with frame
NONE no axes (default)
tickmarks = [m, n, o] alter calibration of the axes
scaling = alter the scaling of the axes
CONSTRAINED same scale on both axes
UNCONSTRAINED different scale on the axes (default)
numpoints = n set number of points to be plotted according to direction
(default is $25^2 = 625$)
orientation = [θ,ϕ] set viewpoint direction (θ,ϕ are given in degrees)
Default values are: $\theta = 45°$, $\phi = 45°$. Other values are: **FISHEYE, NORMAL,
ORTHOGONAL**
shading = set colour scale
The following models are available: **XYZ, XY, Z, ZGRAYSCALE, ZHUE,
NONE**

print(*expr1, expr2,...*)
    prints the expression (*expr1* ...). String constants must be enclosed between single opening quotes.

proc(*var*)... **end;**
    describes a procedure.

product(*term,var=varmin.. varmax*)
    calculates finite and infinite products.

Re(*z*)
    calculates the real part of a complex number.

read *'filename'*
    reads a text file (*filename*) with *Maple* commands.

rhs(*equation*)
    determines the right side of an equation.

row(*matrix, n*)
    provides the *n*th row of a matrix (*matrix*). (Command from the **linalg** package.)

save *expr1, expr2, ..., 'filename'*
    saves the expression (*expr1* ...) to the file (*filename*).

sec(*x*)
    calculates the secant function (sec *x*).

seq(*expr, domain*)
    outputs a sequence of expressions in the declared domain.

series(*f,{var, var0, varh}*)
    calculates the series power of function *f* at the location *var0* up to the highest power *varh*.

simplify(*expr*)
    simplifies an expression.

sin(*x*)
    calculates the sine function (sin *x*).

solve(*{ls = rs...}, var*)
    solves an equation or a set of equations for the declared solution variables.

sqrt(*x*)
    calculates the square root of *x*.

stack(*matrix1, matrix2*)
combines two matrices rowwise into one. (Command from the **linalg** package.)

submatrix(*matrix, z1..z2, s1..s2*)
provides the partial matrix of a matrix (*matrix*). (Command from the **linalg** package.)

subs(*expr1=expr2, expr3*)
in the third expression replaces the first with the second.

sum(*term, var=varmin.. varmax*)
calculates finite and infinite sums.

swapcol(*matrix, s1, s2*)
swaps two columns of a matrix (*matrix*). (Command from the **linalg** package.)

table(*option, list*)
describes a table.

tan(*x*)
calculates the tangent function (tan *x*).

tcoeff(*expr, var*)
determines the lowest coefficient of the variable *var* in the expression *expr*.

transpose(*matrix*)
calculates the transpose of a matrix. (Command from the **linalg** package.)

union
union of sets.

vector(*list*)
assigns vectors. The list (*list*) contains the coordinates. (Command from the **linalg** package.)

vector(*n*)
defines vectors. For this the number of coordinates (*n*) must be provided. (Command from the **linalg** package.)

with(*name*)
loads a command package.

Appendix C Solutions

The solutions given are not the mathematical solutions but a correct input for *Maple*.

C.1   Solutions for chapter 1

```
1. > ifactor(2^45-1);
2. > sqrt(17)*sqrt(68);
3. > ln(335);
   > simplify(");
   > evalf(");
4. > log[4](2048);
   > simplify(");
5. > sin(convert(135*degrees,radians));
   > evalf(");
6. > Re(5-5*I);
7. > Im(5-5*I);
8. > abs(5-5*I);
9. > arctan(5/-5);
```

C.2   Solutions for chapter 2

```
1. > expand((x+y-17)*(x^2+14*x-37));
2. > coeff(expand((x+y-17)*(x^2+14*x-37)),y);
3. > degree(expand((x+y-17)*(x^2+14*x-37)),x);
4. > factor(3*x^5-5*x^4-27*x^3+45*x^2-1200*x+2000,I);
5. > normal((x^2-5*x+6)/(x-3));
```

For the remaining problems the following variable is defined:
FRACTION=((x-5)(x+14)/((x+11)(x-17))

```
6. > expand(FRACTION);
7. > expand(numer(FRACTION)/expand(denom(FRACTION)));
8. > convert(FRACTION,parfrac,x);
```

C.3   Solutions for chapter 3

```
1. > f:=x->x*sin(x);
2. > WT:=[seq([x*Pi/6,f(x*Pi/6)],x=0..12)];
3. > op(5,WT);
4. > op(2,op(4,WT));
```

C.4   Solutions for chapter 4

```
1. > solve(15*x^2-2*x-8=0,x);
2. > solve(x^4-4*x^3=17*x^2+16*x+84,x);
3. > solve(sqrt(x+2)-1=sqrt(x));
     Test:
   > simplify(subs(x=1/4,sqrt(x+2)-1));
   > simplify(subs(x=1/4,sqrt(x)));
4. > solve(2*(cos(x))^2+3*cos(x)+1=0,x);
```
5. Here only the left side is to be evaluated.
```
   > simplify(subs(x=2,abs(x^2-10*x+20)));
   > simplify(subs(x=4,abs(x^2-10*x+20)));
   > simplify(subs(x=6,abs(x^2-10*x+20)));
   > simplify(subs(x=8,abs(x^2-10*x+20)));
```

C.5   Solutions for chapter 5

All solutions are determined with `linalg`.
Definition of the matrices:
```
> M1:=matrix(3,3,[1,2,3,4,5,6,7,8,9]);
> M2:=matrix(3,3,[1,0,1,0,1,0,0,1,1]);
```

```
1. > evalm(M1+M2);
2. > evalm(M1&*M2);
3. > transpose(M1);
4. > det(M2);
5. > inverse(M2);
6. > solve({2*x+8y+14*z=178,  7*x+  y+ 4*z= 74,
   >            4*x+7*y+24z= 77},{x,y,z});
   or
   > linsolve([[2,8,14],[7,1,4],[4,7,1]],[178,74,77]);
```

C.6   Solutions for chapter 6

```
1. > plot(sin(x)/x,x=0.001..2*Pi,
   >        title='sin(x)/x');
2. > plot([2*cos(t),2*sin(t),t=0..Pi]);
3. > plot3d([2*cos(t)*sin(u),2*sin(t)*sin(u),
   >          2*cos(u)[,t=0..2*Pi,u=0..Pi/2);
```

C.7   Solutions for chapter 7

```
1. > diff(E^(4-x^2)*cos(x),x);
2. > diff(E^(4-x^2)*sin(y),x,y);
3. > int(sqrt(x^2-2*x+5),x);
4. > int(sqrt(x^2-2*x+5),x=0..5);
   > evalf(");
5. > dsolve(diff(f(x),x)-x^2*(f(x))^2=x^2,
   >          f(x),explicit);
```

C.8   Solutions for chapter 8

1.
```
> KD:=proc(TERM,A,B)
> local N,E,W;
> N:=solve(TERM=0,x);
> print(' The zero positions are : ');
> print(N);
> E:=solve(diff(TERM,x)=0,x);
> print(' The extreme positions are : ');
> print(E);
> W:=solve(diff(TERM,x$2)=0,x);
> print(' The turning positions are : ');
> print(W);
> plot(TERM,x=A..B);
> end;
```

Bibliography

[1]   Char, Bruce, Geddes, Keith, Gonnet, Gaston, Leong, Beton, Monagan, Michael, Watt, Stephen, *Maple* V Language Reference Manual — Springer-Verlag, New York Berlin Heidelberg 1991

[2]   Char, Bruce, Geddes, Keith, Gonnet, Gaston, Leong, Beton, Monagan, Michael, Watt, Stephen, *Maple* V Library Reference Manual — Springer-Verlag, New York Berlin Heidelberg 1991

[3]   Char, Bruce, Geddes, Keith, Gonnet, Gaston, Leong, Beton, Monagan, Michael, Watt, Stephen, First Leaves: A Tutorial Introduction to *Maple* V — Springer-Verlag, New York Berlin Heidelberg 1992

[4]   Monagan, Michael, Programming in *Maple*: The Basics — ETH Zentrum, Zürich 1992

[5]   Burkhardt, Werner, Erste Schritte mit Mathematica — Springer-Verlag, Berlin Heidelberg 1993

[6]   Davenport, J.H., Siret, Y., Tournier, E., Computer Algebra — Academic Press, London 1988

[7]   Leupold, Wilhelm *et al.*, Lehr- und Übungsbuch Mathematik Band III. — VEB Fachbuchverlag, Leipzig 1983

Index